Values in the Workplace

THE **mananam** SERIES
(Mananam–Sanskrit for "Reflection upon the Truth")

Listed in Sequence of Publication

THE **mananam** SERIES

Values in the Workplace

CHINMAYA PUBLICATIONS
CHINMAYA MISSION WEST PUBLICATIONS DIVISION

Chinmaya Publications
560 Bridgetown Pike, Langhorne, PA 19053, USA
(888) CMW-READ; (215) 396-0390
www.chinmayamission.org

Chinmaya Mission West
P.O. Box 129, Piercy, CA 95587, USA
(707) 247-3488
www.chinmayamission.org

Central Chinmaya Mission Trust
Sandeepany Sadhanalaya
Saki Vihar Road
Mumbai 400 072, India
www.chinmayamission.com

Editorial Team:
Editorial Advisor: *H.H. Swami Tejomayananda*
Consulting Editor: *Swami Shantananda*
Series Editors: *Margaret Dukes, Neena Dev, Rashmi Mehrotra*
Production & Permissions Manager: *Arun Mehrotra*
Production & Editorial Assistant: *David Dukes*

Library of Congress Control Number: 2008906251
ISBN: 978-1-880687-96-3

Printed in the United States of America

Contents

xi

Preface

"In and through all his actions — physical, mental, and intellectual—man can bring forth the expression of his true dharma, his divine Essence."

— *Swami Chinmayananda*

Values are the foundation upon which we base all our actions. They determine how we interact in the world. The quality of our thoughts and actions, and therefore our character, is determined by the types of values we respect and practice. If we base our actions on dharma (righteous conduct) we bring prosperity and harmony to ourselves and to the world around us. As we practice these values we invoke them more and more within ourselves and our true goodness gradually unfolds.

We have many fields of action in which to exercise these *dhārmika* values. One of the fields of action is our workplace. And here continually, many decisions and choices need to be made. But making the right decision may not always be easy or pleasant. The factor that governs our ability to make a good choice is clarity of thinking. In order to achieve this clarity, spiritual practice, *sādhanā*, is of utmost importance. This is when the *dhārmika* principles we have embraced become the foundation upon which our decisions are based. There is nothing wrong in earning a living if it is earned based on universal values such as honesty, integrity, and truth. Only then can lasting peace and happiness be achieved.

Part One in this book points out that values need to be understood and practiced. Commitment to ethical standards, such as honesty and living the Golden Rule, generates a climate of trust that helps us achieve success honorably in business. Thus the workplace becomes a field to practice and live our highest values.

Transforming ourselves through work is the subject of Part Two. The writers describe the dilemmas that some of us face in the workplace and they offer strategies to deal with them. They define genuine success as staying true to our higher purpose and convictions. The kind of attitude with which we work largely determines how we spiritually evolve.

In Part Three the writers define the qualities of a good leader. They show how accomplished leaders strongly live their values and clearly articulate an inspired vision in others. Many leaders are now recognizing the importance of moral intelligence and how it helps to achieve a balance within oneself and work in a spirit of dedication.

In Part Four, the Workplace, we learn how some companies remain strong and viable because of their adherence to core (*dhārmika*) values. Examples are given of workplaces that changed their way of doing business beyond maximizing profits. They realized that maintaining the highest ethical standards was not only the right thing to do but also produced the best company with excellent results for all.

Most of us define success by what we value, our material possessions. As a result we are often disappointed. However, the authors in this book show how lasting success and happiness is gained by living our values in the workplace and at home. They provide practical advice and exercises to help us strengthen our own moral competency and effectiveness.

The Editors

PART ONE

The Foundation

*Values are the roots from where
an organization continuously gets
its supply as well as grounding.
Build on them!*

Jim Collins

People will be able to sustain a virtuous life only when the values and virtues they uphold are dedicated for inner purification, God-Realization, or devotion to God. Then only can one persevere in the midst of obstacles and hindrances. There has to be a high altar of dedication. Such an altar in life will alter our life. We call ourselves the roof and crown of creation. Therefore, we must prove ourselves worthy of this high calling.

The rich must look after the welfare of the poor and make sure they also become prosperous. The superior must protect the inferior and the more powerful must look after the weaker. Such actions alone will add value to our lives. Otherwise we will add years to our lives and not life to our years. Our own lives must be vibrant so that they are a blessing to others and to ourselves.

Swami Tejomayananda

I

Human Values and Their Value

by Swami Atmashraddhananda

Krishnan, the young cricket fan, leapt with joy when he learnt the news that his team had won the cricket tournament. He had been away the whole day and had not been able to keep track of the game. He came to know of this news only when he returned home in the evening. He called up Sudhir, his friend, asking him to come for a treat to celebrate the victory. "But," responded Sudhir, "you are misinformed. It is not our team but the other team which has won the tournament." Disappointed and sad, Krishnan simply hung up and was sore for the next two days.

The message is clear: Krishnan was jubilant not because of the cricket-victory as such but because he had assumed that it was his team, which had won the tournament. The moment he discovered that his team was not the winner he lost all his interest. He was no longer jubilant and happy.

Shri Ramakrishna's well-known story about the lady sweeping the courtyard also drives home the same fact very well. While she was sweeping the courtyard, the lady heard a messenger saying that there was an accident on the roadside and someone was badly injured. She just made a nodding sound in response and continued sweeping. A little later the messenger returned and reported excitedly that the person hurt was her son. At this she stood up, baffled and stunned, her broom fell from her hands, and she fainted on the ground.

In both cases, the reactions are born from a sense of belonging. The losing of the tournament and the injured person made no difference until they were found connected to oneself. Obviously things affect us only when they concern us. Though we live amidst values, our greatest value is our self. When this self is disturbed, we feel disturbed.

It is reported about Albert Einstein that when the preparations for the atomic bomb were under way, he was supposed to have remarked, "If this [atomic bomb] becomes successful, the Americans will say that I am an American and the Germans will say I am German. But if it becomes unsuccessful, the Americans will say I am a German and the Germans will say I am an American."

This is a humorous way of stating a great truth. It only shows the human tendency to own what is good and commendable and disown what is harmful and useless.

Vedanta discovered this long, long ago. Much of discussion in Vedantic texts is about the real nature of self. The question of "self" is all right but then, what is self? The sages of the Upanishads dived deep into the structure of human personality and discovered the truth that man is essentially divine. His self is divine, eternal. Man is not just a collection of sensory experiences or intellectual exercises or emotional needs. Nor is it that man's deepest need lies in fulfilling these aspects of his personality. Man's greatest need lies in knowing that he is divine, ever-fulfilled, ever-calm. His physical and emotional and intellectual attainments cannot satisfy his spiritual aspirations. Only when a man experiences his spiritual nature, he becomes free from all conflicts, stress and fear. He then becomes unshakable and fully established in all the noble virtues of life.

How Values are Born

Though this truth about us may be true, what we see or experience in our daily life is nowhere indicative of this. Generally we live among values, which are monetary, professional and mundane. We are surrounded and guided by a number of worldly values. We value money. We value our property and bank balance. We value our looks. We value our pleasures and comforts. We value our near and dear ones. We value our personal and social reputation. And if anything goes to harm what we thus value, we fight against it. We have laid out many well-thought rules for protecting and amplifying what we value.

This sense of value is, however, based on our notion about ourselves. It is from the self that our notion of what is valuable (to us) comes. We think this is what we are — a mixed bag of physical and emotional and social values. Our idea of our "self" is so limited and so gross. That is why there is so much clinging to all matters related to this. We tell ourselves that we need money and reputation and try to close the issue there.

Though our ordinary experience tells us that this is what we need, thank God man cannot remain satisfied with it. He keeps thinking and wondering about life in its deeper dimensions. He asks what is life and how to live it. He wants to know more about himself and others and the power that activates and controls everyone and everything. He searches for something deeper than what is available on the surface. He seeks lasting happiness and peace. This is what has led the mystics of the world to discover the truth of human personality: the ever-present divine within. This core, again, they found, was non-different from the Ultimate Reality of life.

Man has a spiritual core and from that comes all his moral and spiritual values. Shri Ramakrishna used to refer to this spiritual core as a digit one and all the rest as zero. If a bank note has only ten zeros, it is useless. But if the same check has a digit at the beginning — 1 or 2 or 5 and so on — it has great value.

Most people today have reduced themselves to mere biological, economic, political or social units. They thus value only those things that confirm their biological, economic, political or social worth. But what happens when we value ourselves as spiritual beings? We begin valuing spiritual values. These values are the values that make us human beings truly human.

What are spiritual values? The blanket term used to denote spiritual values is dharma. Unlike its popular translation, this well-known term does not mean religion. Dharma is derived from the root *dhṛ*, to hold. "That which holds life together is called dharma," says a celebrated definition. In other words, those virtues, attitudes, principles and practices that keep us together is dharma. It protects us from moral disintegration and decay. Since dharma is based on our inner being, it defies all attempts to outsmart it. However clever one may be, one cannot ignore it. Dharma is the very basis of life.

Developing Human Values

If dharma is the basis of life, where is the need to develop it? Is it not already there, being the basis? Yes, it is already there but it mostly lies uncultivated. It is like the seeds that have not been cultivated. One may have good seeds but unless they are sown, watered, provided sunshine and protection, they cannot grow. To cultivate dharma is to channel our attitudes into higher, nobler directions. Says a verse from the Upanishad:

> The stream of tendencies flowing through good and evil channels is to be directed by self-effort along the good path. When it has entered the evil path, it is to be turned towards the good path.[1]

Self-effort is required for developing dharma. It does not happen automatically for the simple reason that we have both the channels open before us and our present state of being can turn either way. We have seeds of good and evil right within us. These seeds are getting watered and nourished in many ways. If we do not cultivate the seeds of goodness, of dharma, the seeds of evil or *adharma* get cultivated (*adharma* or evil means violation of our spiritual nature).

People in today's world think that dharma is outdated. Yet, at the same time, they expect everyone they deal with, to be trustworthy and honest. Does anyone want a fraudulent government, scheming colleagues and unfaithful brothers and sisters?

Let us not make any mistake about it.

There is that account of a child who was being told a night-time story. "A battle goes on inside people," his granny told him. "The battle is between two wolves inside us all. One is Evil — anger, hatred, violence, confusion, and selfishness. The other one is Good represented by self-control, patience, contentment, forgiveness and unselfishness." The child thought about this for a moment and asked his granny, "Which wolf wins?" The granny replied, "The one you feed."

To feed good "wolf" is to cultivate dharma. The struggle is between self-control and self-indulgence. The more our battle for self-control is won, the nearer we are to our deepest Self and the core of dharma.

There have always been debates and disagreements as to what constitutes "good" and "bad," the terms having wide-ranging connotations. Time, place, purpose, cultural practices and religious sanctions add different colors to the term "good" and "bad." Swami Vivekananda was, however, very direct and clear in this matter. As to what is moral and immoral, he said, "That which is selfish is immoral, and that which is unselfish is moral."[2]

Conclusion

Our values are based on our self-concept. If we think ourselves material, our values too become material. If we think ourselves as spiritual entities, our values too become spiritual. If we accept our spiritual nature, we need to cultivate virtues such as patience, equality, forgiveness, honesty, and so on. Dharma is the spiritual principle that holds us together. If we violate it, we go against the very nature of life, against ourselves. In doing evil, we injure others and also ourselves. We get what we give. If we give love, it returns. If we send hatred, it returns, too.

Dharma is simply tearing off the veil of false identity that hides our true Self. The Self is the foundation of all unselfishness. The nearer we are to our core, the more unselfish we are because the same Self resides in all. Only when we understand this do we discover the real reason for becoming good. The most compelling reason for becoming good, and not harming others, lies in our being. Our "being" is as much present in others as in us. The divinity present in everyone does not have any "variety" or plurality. It is singular, one. This feeling of oneness is the basis of our reason for practice of kindness, love and other virtues.

All human values originate from the very fabric of our being — the infinite dimension called *ātman*. And it is there that their value lies, intrinsically and truly.

FOOTNOTES:

1   *Muktikopaniṣad*, 2:5.6.
2   *The Complete Works of Swami Vivekananda*, 1:11.

II

Holistic Management

by Swami Tejomayananda

Management implies many factors: a manager, the resources to be managed, the goal to be achieved and the methods to be employed. It is very clear that the manager has to be a human being; because a machine does not manage things by itself; a human being has to install the machine. First of all, a manager has to learn to manage himself; only then can he manage others. He has to have a good value system from where he can draw his strength and function efficiently.

Resources to be Managed

All the things to be managed fall under three categories — man, materials, and money. Without building up and managing monetary resources we cannot function successfully. The material to be managed may vary. In business, the material will depend on the kind of product to be generated. In educational institutions, it is of an entirely different kind. In a household, it is different still.

A renowned professor of management told me that ultimately all management boils down to the management of "man." And there are only two types of men — those who have difficulties and those who are difficult. It is perhaps easier to manage people who are difficult, because you already know they are difficult.

The Goal

A person has to manage the resources for a particular purpose. The goals may vary depending on whether he is managing a household, an institution, a political party, and so on. However the wider goal has to be kept in mind. If the people, for whose happiness and welfare we claim to function, are themselves exploited or made miserable, it defeats the very purpose. We talk about industrialization, globalization, liberalization, and so on, but in the process, all the nations are reduced to the state of markets only — either a good market, or a potential market. Most people are reduced to the status of consumers, only to be exploited.

Methods of Management

We hear of many systems of management, like the American model, the Japanese model, the Indian model, the Eastern model, Indian ethos, and so on. There are many systems, but I don't think any system is foolproof. The success or failure of the system ultimately depends on the person who is going to manage. In the political arena, for example, a dictator may happen to be very democratic and benign like Bhagawan Ramchandraji, while democracy may see the emergence of great dictators. Sometimes, in a democratic system, the people elect their own persecutor!

Values in Management

We may know many theories of management, but without values they have no value. We talk of value-based management, value-based business, value-based education, value-based politics — we know it all. The problem is that we do not implement it. We do not live our values. There is corruption everywhere; even in religion, there are fake *saṁnyāsī*! It has become a way of life. Now we call it "co-operation," not corruption. All of

11

us know in our heart of hearts that everything has to be value-based, but there is always a feeling that it cannot be done. Some thought has to be given to this.

There are four kinds of people:

1. Those who are unscrupulous and have no values at all.
2. Those who have values but are not able to live up to them.
3. Those who accept values, but feel that it is not possible to practice them in today's world and so consider them irrelevant.
4. Those who have wrong values in life.

If one has no values at all, one's life will be valueless and this type of life is not worth living. If one has the values but is not able to live up to them, the only thing one has to do is to become strong. And if a person has the wrong values, God help him!

It is the third kind of person I am concerned about now, because his attitude is very insidious and dangerous. Are values really irrelevant today? Is it true that nobody respects values?

A little thinking shows that all of us respect values, and respect only those people who respect values and are able to follow them. There is no doubt about it. The only problem with us is that we want to see these values in someone else! I may earn money by whatever means, fair or foul, but I want my accountant to be very honest, my servant to be honest, and my security person to be honest! I may speak the truth or not, but I want others to speak only the truth. But the power of truth is such that even when a person tells a lie, that person claims that he is telling the truth, because the lie, the untruth, has no face to show, it goes in the name of truth only.

Another interesting thing we observe is that the mafia — or the underworld doing dishonest business — flourishes, because even in their dishonest business there is honesty. The business may be dishonest, but among themselves a perfect unwritten law exists. Sharing of profits and money is done as per their given word.

One of the greatest assets in business is credibility. Once it is lost, everything is lost. You may cheat once, twice, but if your credibility is lost, you are finished.

A businessman who was teaching his son said, "Son, in business two things are very important: one is integrity and the other wisdom. Integrity means that once you have made a commitment, a promise, you must fulfill that, even if you have to suffer a loss for it sometimes. Wisdom is to avoid giving any promise, making any commitment!"

For instance, take match-fixing in sports, does anyone like that? No. Why not? It is because something within us revolts against it. There is an innate sense of values in us. We may applaud a person for great achievements, but we respect a person only for what he is. What one has and what one is are totally different things.

The great values of life never become irrelevant and ultimately they alone succeed. Thus, lasting success is achieved by hard work, honesty, loyalty, integrity; it is achieved by these values alone and not by anything else.

Sacrifice vs. Compromise

There are two ways of living: one is called *compromise* and the other *sacrifice*. In both, a person has to renounce something. God has made life in such a way that without renouncing you cannot live here. Inhaling is possible only when you exhale also. If you say you won't exhale, you cannot live. Without giving up the lower, you cannot get the higher; you cannot grow. In compromise man gives up higher values and ideals for lower gains. In sacrifice he gives up lower things for the higher. Renunciation is involved in both.

A man of compromises has never become an ideal anywhere in this world; only a man of sacrifice becomes an ideal, a leader worthy of respect. This is a historical truth. So our thinking must be, "I have to renounce anyway, either this or that. What am I going to renounce? When I renounce my ideals, my values, it means I am selling myself, selling my soul. On the other hand, by refusing to compromise, I may suffer a little, undergo some hardships, and forego some comforts. So what? One has to pay a price for everything. So be it."

Some people come to me in their old age, having retired from high positions, with all the comforts life can offer, but suffering from sleepless nights. There is a small thing called conscience. You continue to keep quiet, but for how long? All those memories of past misdeeds are haunting them. The price has to be paid in this manner. In compromise there will be immediate pleasure, no doubt, but pain follows in its wake. It is better to die once than to die of guilt moment to moment. Only when that type of conviction comes is it possible to sacrifice.

Holistic Management

In holistic management, "holistic" means "whole" as well as "holy," that is, purifying. It includes all the factors discussed so far. Without this vision and without these values no management can be successful. Doubting these values and thinking they are irrelevant is more dangerous than not having them at all. This world is very straightforward. Fire seems to say, "Touch me not, I am hot. If you touch me you will be burnt." If you follow the rule, the rule itself will protect you but if you don't, be ready for the consequences.

Strangely enough, man is not afraid of committing sins; he is only afraid of being caught. He is not afraid of action; rather, he is afraid of consequences. If you do not want the consequences, then why do you indulge in that action? There is a beautiful saying in Sanskrit, paraphrased as follows: "People want the results of meritorious deeds, like happiness, and so forth, but they do not want to do meritorious deeds. They do not want the consequences of sins but they commit sins deliberately!"

Now the choice is yours. That is the beauty of human life; we can become *devatā* (divine beings), or we can become *dānava* (demons); both are possible. If we want to be happy, there is no choice other than to follow a proper value system. Nobody wants to live a life of suffering. We have to stand up and try our best, so that at least we can say that we tried. Of course, when we try, it is a trying period, but it will lead to joy and a great sense of fulfillment. It is immaterial whether others appreciate and applaud or not. We would have lived a life of right values. That is the most important thing.

Values are never irrelevant; they are independent of time and space. Values are not for others alone — they are first for us, then for others. Be afraid of the consequences of your actions. Everybody has to renounce; don't live a life of compromise; make it one of sacrifice — the choice is yours. This is holistic management of yourself and thereby of others.

III

A Dialogue on Values, Ethics, and Morality

by Swami Chinmayananda

Q: Many people today are talking about values. How would you define values?

A: A thing by itself has no value. For instance, a piece of wood lying at the roadside is worthless. But suppose a carpenter gives it some shape and makes a toy out of it, then it has value. A piece of rusting iron has no value, but if a blacksmith heats it, shapes it and adds a wooden handle, it becomes a knife and has value. Thus, the thing plus your effort gives it value. Raw materials by themselves have no value but when we use our knowledge and add effort then it becomes something valuable and useful to society.

We cannot get values by merely listening to or reading about them. We have to reflect on them, work on creating the right values and then put them into practice, just as our health will not improve by just listening to a health-expert. We must make an effort to discipline ourselves to eat properly and exercise. In the same way, unless we begin integrating the higher values of life that all the great masters, prophets, and saints have been expounding upon, nothing will happen.

When we do live the right values, such as love, tenderness, mercy, kindness, forgiveness, and so on, we are able to meet all the challenges of life. And by developing these noble virtues within us we become fearless; ready to face any challenge without being crushed or weighed down by them.

Q: What are these values based upon?

A: These values are the ethical and moral values prescribed by religion and the eternal truths of life. The world may change, but the eternal values will always remain the same. There are some fundamental things in the world that continue to exist and function in the same way, however ancient they may be. About the nineteenth century we discovered electricity; that does not mean that electricity was not there in the first century. Electricity was always there as a fundamental energy in the cosmos. The gravitational force existed, and was functioning in the same way as it is today, even before Newton discovered it.

Similarly, in human life, there are certain unquestionable fundamental values which, when lived, make us more capable of facing the world, whether it is riddled with endless tragedies or filled with joy. These values govern our inner health and are called eternal values by the scriptures.

A student who studies various religions may find that one religion emphasizes one set of ideals over another. But if one thinks about them intelligently, one discovers that the fundamental principles behind them are the same. Just as two doctors may prescribe seemingly different prescriptions to the same patient, for the same disease, and yet those who understand medicine know that they have the same effect on illness. It is only in the details that they appear different.

Similarly, the ethical and moral values that religions prescribe are rules of conduct by which we can integrate our personality and gain inner health. It is by this method alone that we may be able to enjoy the world more and develop the strength and courage to meet all our problems in life. It is true, no doubt, that there are only a few in society who live these great values but those few grow to such a stature that they lead the world with an irresistible spiritual power. It is always such people of heroic inner personality, who have been guiding the generations and initiating a new civilization of integrated head and heart in the world.

17

Q: Do the values of life have intrinsic worth or do they have instrumental worth? In other words, is the value valuable in itself or is it an instrument to achieving something else that a value is valuable?

A: A value is valuable only in relationship to achievements. It is instrumental. It is not absolute. Only *Brahman,* the Supreme Reality, has absolute value.

Q: You mean, *Brahman* is the only intrinsic value?

A: Yes, *Brahman* is the only intrinsic value. All others are instrumental or contributory to reaching that highest intrinsic value. By pursuing negative thoughts and deeds we go away from That. By pursuing positive values we go toward That. Therefore the values to be acquired by the seeker are only to take him to that intrinsic value, the absolute value that is *Brahman.*

Q: Swamiji how would you define the words ethics and morality?

A: The right and healthy values of life that we maintain in ourselves comprise ethics, while morality is manifest in our behavior concerning the outer world. There are either ethical or unethical thoughts, but immoral thoughts are not possible. There can be moral or immoral action but there is no such thing as ethical action.

The word "ethics" is used in a subjective sense while "morality" is used in relation to the discipline of one's behavior in the world. Therefore one speaks of ethical values and moral behavior. Unless we develop ethical values we cannot live a moral life. Ethics is something we have to cultivate in ourselves, and its expression in the world becomes morality. An ethically bad person cannot be morally good. A moral person acts from the ethical values that he has cultivated in himself

Q: What is the highest moral truth?

A: Love is the greatest morality given to humanity and hence Love Thyself is the greatest moral injunction that scriptures and the Vedanta tirelessly repeat. But unless the student is prepared to receive this grand advice, he is apt to misunderstand it as advice to love the body and to cater to all low thoughts and ideas.

Love thyself does not mean loving the body or obeying the mind and intellect meekly. The body, mind, and intellect are gross matter envelopments that have come to seemingly limit the illimitable supreme Consciousness, which is the real Self in us all. Through our wrong identification with the false matter envelopments, we have projected ourselves into the outer world as a separate ego, and doubts on morality and spirituality have come to confuse us.

The shifting of our identification to the real Self is to live automatically the highest moral and spiritual life. This is accomplished through love, in love, as love. Love alone is the law and the life of the Self. Self-realization is the experience of love in its absolute nature. Raise thyself. When you have raised yourself to love your Self the most, thereafter you know nothing but love for the world. There is no greater moral truth than love.

IV

Ethics and Personal Growth

by William Damon

Real ethics cannot be understood as a disconnected set of rules. Ethical behavior is wholly embedded in a person's larger sense of self and society. What kind of a person do I want to be? How can I become that person? What do I want to accomplish in life? What do I want to leave behind! In the answers to these questions, people find compelling reasons to act ethically.

When understood as a central component of a person's identity, instead of as a separate rule system externally forced on the person, ethics acquires a positive rather than constraining quality. It then becomes possible to see how strong ethics can help us achieve our loftiest goals. Ethical acts become part of the tool kit for solving life's problems and expanding personal frontiers. Along with affiliated character virtues such as honesty and humility, ethical acts keep us on course in the direction that best serves the long-term interests of everyone in the picture — ourselves, our companies, as well as society and the world at large.

The key to this understanding is to focus on the big questions — who I am and what I want to accomplish in the highest sense — even amid the most severe pressures of competition and crisis in everyday business life. This is easier said than done, however, but it is a capacity that can be cultivated over time, much like any useful skill or habit. Many business leaders acquire this capacity through religious or spiritual faith. In our study, for example, we found that a majority of the business leaders interviewed were people of devout faith, even though they often avoided expressing religious views in their workplaces. Faith is one way — not the only way, but a powerful one — to keep a steady ethical compass amid temptations and pressures to compromise.

McDonald Williams, the CEO and chairman of the board at Trammel Crow Company, the huge Dallas real-estate outfit, recalled the times in his life when he wondered whether he was going to make it economically. One instance was back in the early seventies, during a severe recession. He was still a young man then, with four children and a mortgage on his home. "I'm busted," he said, "and you talk about a moment of truth, but what came to me at that time was probably as close to an epiphany in business as I've ever had, and that is, 'Wait a minute, why did you come? You came here because of the people and the values. Had those things changed? No. External business environments have changed. We're in trouble, but the reasons I came persist, and I can make a difference in this environment.'" Williams survived the crisis of the early seventies and prospered, only to watch his company fall back into another economic downturn in the late eighties. He explained the role of his faith in keeping a steady grip on his sense of purpose and his ethical values during these difficult periods:

> Values get tested on tough times, not good times. And I think that my faith helped, because once I went through that first time, I said, "Wait a minute, I'm not my net worth. I'm not my business reputation." And I never lost sleep going through the hardest times. We had guys who weren't going to sleep and their marriages were breaking up and they were doing things that they shouldn't be doing. But I think faith for me gave me an internal perspective....
>
> My faith was more relevant to my business in tough times than anything else because then your values really were square in your face. Are you going to live them or not? Are you going to look beyond the moment for a longer time frame? Who are you? Are you just your job? Are you just your career? Or are

you just your reputation? Or are you just your net worth? ... I mean, they are important to me, I can't deny that. But I think faith helped me, in that moment to have perspective.

Ethics and Faith

In a similar vein, Dickie Sykes, the assistant vice president and equal employment officer of AMEC Construction Management, integrates all her personal goals around her belief in the higher purpose of her vocation. For Sykes, this has the ultimate spiritual as well as personal significance: "I have a strong spiritual foundation, and this isn't for everyone. I don't think people should impose their beliefs on others, especially in the work environment. But I can say personally that having a strong conviction that everything is going to work out — number one, it keeps you calm; number two, it keeps you from being desperately afraid of the unknown, to the point where you're immobilized."

Sykes's purpose is to promote opportunity for all in the workplace, a purpose that is linked directly to the ethical standard of fairness: "What I'm trying to accomplish, basically, is to ensure that we have equity and fairness on all of our project sites and in our internal work environment, ensuring that minorities and women get treated fairly and equitably in the workforce. Also, to ensure that small, minority- [owned], and women-owned businesses get treated fairly in our construction projects across the country. All of it has worth and meaning. When someone comes up to you and says, 'Dickie, you helped put my children through college' — no amount of money gives you that feeling. It's indescribable to know that what you do changes people's lives."

Many people who succeed in business over the long haul have refused to compartmentalize their ethical and financial goals. They have a sense of wholeness in their approach to every aspect of their lives: indeed, this is the very meaning of the word *integrity*. The wholeness is made possible by their dedication to the higher purpose that defines what they are trying to accomplish and, ultimately, who they are and what kind of person they strive to be. As do Williams and Sykes, many businesspeople look to faith as a way of preserving their integrity when ethical challenges arise, although other leaders find secular beliefs to keep themselves ethically oriented.

Richard Jacobsen is a real-estate developer and property manager in Northern California. He is consciously aware of the intimate connections between his business goals and his determination to live an ethical life. A devout Mormon, Jacobsen is one of the many business leaders with whom we spoke who centers his multiple aspirations around his religious faith. In his interview, he was highly articulate about the ways in which all of a person's motives — financial, moral, personal, and spiritual — must join together for true success.

Jacobsen's endorsement of a "whole person" approach to business is right in line with the message that we heard from almost all of the business leaders in our study: "I think it's really a whole, it's not one thing or another. It's the whole, sort of a holistic approach. You're not just well if you're physically well, but you're well if you're mentally well, emotionally well, physically well, and spiritually well. I'm successful if I'm successful in my business and in my home and in my community and in my church. All of those aspects have to be cultivated together. The measure of success is not one or the other but all of them taken together."

Ethics, Character, and Integrity

The essence of the whole person is character, for it is character that gives a person "wholeness," that is, integrity. Character is composed of such virtues as honesty, which points the way to the ethical standards that enable a person to live a moral life. As mentioned here and in previous chapters, honesty is a primary ethical standard for any person in business, as is a commitment to the Golden Rule, because these standards create the climate of trust required for lasting business relationships.

The other character virtue central to enduring success is humility. In his interview, Jacobsen articulated the connection between humility, strong ethical values, and lasting business success: "My experience in business — I mean, my partner says, 'Always sell short on arrogance.' We have guys show up in the conference room, and I mean it isn't a very fancy conference room, and they're wearing they['ve] got the expensive briefcase and the Rolex watch and the gold chains around the neck, and they flew in on a Lear jet, and you just put them on the shelf and wait your time and you're going to see that they're going to go up in smoke.... The people that I've seen [who] have really lasted tend to just be built on strong values."

The connectedness of ethical values, character, and purpose argues for a fully integrated rather than a compartmentalized approach to business and life. For educators who would promote high ethical standards in the men and women who go into business, the message is clear: you must emphasize matters of ultimate concern that drive people's noblest purposes and define all our ethical values. For an enlightened vision of success, these will be moral concerns, aimed at service to the world as well as to the self.

For those who choose business as their career — or, more to the point, as their calling — the challenge is to sustain an ethical life amid constant pressures to compromise and sell out. If you see this as a new challenge every time a new pressure arises, you will be certain to fall short of your goal. The pressures are too relentless and the temptations too alluring. You must keep your eye on the ball. And what is the ball? It is, once again, the whole person, the kind of person that you want to be, considered in all its aspects, now and in the future. What kinds of relationships do you wish to have with the people in your life? What contributions do you hope to make to the world in your lifetime? What is the way you wish to be remembered, the part of you that you will leave behind? What is the true source of your deepest satisfaction, and how can you keep aiming at it over the long haul?

For many businesspeople, the quest begins with finding purpose in the work that they do and then achieving success in an honorable manner. But it does not end there. Once success is gained, many believe that it is important to "give back" to the society that supported their work. More than 80 percent of the business leaders in our study said that they were heavily involved in philanthropic giving. Dickie Sykes, the construction company executive mentioned earlier, spoke for many when she summed up the links between her vision of the person she wants to be, her career aspirations, and her desire to "give back" through philanthropy: "I'm a philanthropist at heart. That's the core of who I am. When seeking out a career, for me personally, it was never about how much money I could make. I mean everyone wants to make a decent salary in life. Let's face it, you have to pay bills. But to me it has to be integrated with something that gives back to mankind, something that helps people... because that's who I am and that's what makes me feel good about who I am, just simply being a human being. So it fulfills my own internal philosophy on what I think should be done in society at large."

Philanthropy, like business, can be a noble enterprise. But — and this may come as a surprise — it also shares some of the moral hazards of business, despite its charitable intentions.

V

The Two Paths

by Swami Chinmayananda

The basic knowledge of what is good, and what is bad is known to us all. In spite of it, however, we often choose a path that is not beneficial to our well-being. The Vedantic masters analyzed the reason for such conduct and discovered that there are two distinct paths in life:

- The path of the pleasant (*preyas*)
- The path of the good (*śreyas*)

We are confronted with choosing one of the two paths at every single moment of our lives. The path of the pleasant, as the name suggests, pleases, fascinates, and entices us to take it — now! In contrast, the path of the good may have some unpleasant aspects at first. The path of the pleasant provides immediate pleasure, but later ends up in disappointment and sorrow. The path of the good can be unpleasant at first, but later brings happiness and fulfillment.

The Path of the Pleasant	*The Path of the Good*
• Guided by the demands of the sense organs	• Guided by the subtle intellect
• Temporary joy in the beginning, but sorrow later	• Unpleasant in the beginning, but provides permanent happiness later

The Path of the Pleasant	*The Path of the Good*
• More alluring; caters to the extroverted mind	• Has a hidden beauty, perceived by the introverted mind only
• The path of devolution	• The path of evolution
• The path for the majority of people	• The path followed by only a few people
• Based on sense gratification	• Based on sound knowledge
• Denounced by all religions	• Recommended by all religions

Every action of each living being is motivated by an irresistible instinct to be happy. Happiness seems to be the goal of every struggle and strife in life. Even a worm crawling in refuse wanders about motivated by a hope that it will reach a greater joy. Only in full and absolute contentment all searching will end, and this supreme state of happiness is the goal of all life and the subject of all the scriptures of the world.

It is in this light that the rishis classified all actions into the two categories, that is, with reference to their results. The fruits of action can be of two kinds:

• Those contributing to the ephemeral joys in life
• Those leading to immortal bliss

That is, our efforts can either contribute to some immediate passing material gain, or they can contribute in the long run to our self-nurturing and self-purification.

A corrupt official, through foul and fiendish methods, can excel in accumulating wealth. To the ignorant and sensuous this may appear as an inviting prospect and a welcome success. On the other hand, each of us has the choice to build our lives upon more enduring principles of life such as honesty, piety, mercy, love, and tolerance, and to live for the greater wealth of inner peace and joy.

The weak-minded try to gain immediate flickers of joy by choosing the path of the pleasant, and thus deny themselves the chance to enjoy more lasting happiness later. People of inner strength choose the path of the good, unmindful of any unpleasantness and material privations, ready to suffer in the course of their higher pursuits. They are the ones who emerge as mighty personalities who not only lead fulfilling lives themselves, but also inspire the rest of society toward a more peaceful and happy life.

VI

Taking a Personal Stand
by Howard Gardner, Mihaly Csikszentmihalyi, and William Damon

Sometimes it is not feasible to create a new institution or to re-configure an existing one. To preserve personal integrity, some workers must confront their situations by themselves and either fight against or withdraw from jobs that are no longer aligned with their values.

Occasionally a personal stand can send ripples through the entire society because of the stature of the person involved. A good example is Linus Pauling, who received a Nobel Prize for having developed the quantum mechanical bases of chemistry. Pauling became convinced during the cold war that it was impossible to do good work in science without taking responsibility for its intended or probable use. Hence, he took a leadership role in expanding the realm of science by circulating petitions, leading peaceful marches, and exhorting other scientists not to let themselves be co-opted by projects that supported the development of new weapons. Finally, when he felt he was not making enough headway, Pauling took part in demonstrations that led to his being harassed by police, the FBI, and Congress. The State Department withdrew his passport, thereby handicapping his research on the structure of DNA. A similar path was taken by Benjamin Spock, the pediatrician whose child-rearing guide for years sold more copies than any other book except the Bible. During the same cold war era, Spock felt that it was irresponsible for a physician to worry solely about children's colds or diarrhea when an ever-growing nuclear arsenal threatened to extinguish all life on earth. He tried to work through the American Medical Association, ran as a third-party presidential candidate, and finally took to the streets. Spock also ran into trouble with legal authorities as a result of his deeply held convictions. And there are more controversial examples. In 1971, the security analyst Daniel Ellsberg risked being jailed when he distributed the secret "Pentagon Papers," containing details about U.S. involvement in Vietnam, to a few leading news outlets. And by electing to publish these classified documents, the *New York Times* and the *Washington Post* risked financial and legal penalties.

Putting Ourselves on the Line

A readiness to put ourselves on the line obviously will not always result in positive outcomes for us. No one is irreplaceable, and there seems to be an endless supply of willing practitioners who feel no compulsion to honor the tacit contract that binds them to their domains. On the other hand, resigning need not lead to giving up professional goals. Indeed, the challenge for "domain departers" is to find — or create — institutions or causes that allow them to achieve what is essential to maintain integrity. Two noteworthy examples are John Gardner, who inspired the creation of several influential grassroots civic organizations, and the consumer activist and third-party presidential candidate Ralph Nader, who has challenged conventional governmental and corporate practices repeatedly over the last several decades. Several options are available to scientists who are unhappy about trends within their specialties. For example, they can publish individual critiques. In the area of genetics this is the option followed by insiders like Mae-Wan Ho, or by relative outsiders like Rifkin. They can band together to create an organization like the Council for Responsible Genetics, which has issued the following guideline: "No individual, institution, or corporation should be able to claim ownership over species or varieties of living organisms. Nor should they be able to hold patents on organs, cells, genes, or proteins, whether naturally occurring, genetically altered or otherwise modified."

Students associated with the Pugwash group — a politically oriented scientific association concerned with issues of atomic energy — have developed an oath:

> I promise to work for a better world, where science and technology are used in socially-responsible ways. I will not use my education for any purpose intended to harm human beings or the environment. Throughout my career, I will consider the ethical implications of my work before I take action. While the demands placed upon me may be great, I sign this declaration because I recognize that individual responsibility is the first step on the path to peace.

Finally, raising the ante on these exhortatory moves, it is possible to implement legislation that prohibits certain practices. It would be possible, for instance, to ban for-profit medical or research institutions from pursuing certain kinds of research, such as human cloning, genetic engineering, or the tracing of a target population's genetic profiles. Similarly, regulations might stipulate that only trained physicians could head medical organizations. Such options do not seem likely in the United States today, but practices like desegregation of schools or government funding of medical care for the aging seemed unlikely a century ago.

VII

Finding Value with Values

by Susan Smith Kuczmarski and
Thomas D. Kuczmarski

"To live your life, you have to have a set of values or something that you stand for. I don't know how you manage if you don't have a sense of values from which to base how you operate. It's the guiding light that takes you through the day and is who you are," exclaims Randy Larrimore.

When he became CEO of United Stationers, he gathered his management team together for a three-day session to discuss the future of the company. The newly appointed Fortune 500 leader stepped on stage before a crowd anxious to learn his vision for success. What they heard was Larrimore paraphrasing from Dr. Seuss's book, Oh the Places You'll Go: *"Today is our day. We're off to Great Places! We're off and away! There is fun to be done! There are points to be scored. There are games to be won. Our mountain is waiting. So let's get on our way!" By reading this book, he expressed his values to the group, albeit in a very creative way. He wanted the group to have fun, work hard, and win the game together.*

For Larrimore, values are not rhetorical devices or convenient symbols; values are at the center of any successful business model. "If you have happy associates, they are more likely to better satisfy your customers, who are more likely to develop loyalty to your company and buy more of your product or service," he says. "This will also make the employees happier. I think shareholder value can be driven by a strong set of values within an organization. If you are going to empower people and push decision-making down, and give people a sense of responsibility, then you have to have a strong set of values — so that you are confident they are going to make the decisions that will benefit the company overall."

Unquestionably, Larrimore finds value in values. They permeate, guide, and inform decision-making everywhere within his company.

Living "The Golden Rule"

In a business world feared for its complexity, Randy Larrimore operates according to one simple rule — The Golden Rule.

"My personal values are based around treating other people as I would like to be treated," he says. "Everything is based around that. That leads to treating people with dignity and respect no matter what their station in life. I think it also leads to a strong belief in honesty and integrity."

In college, Larrimore worked for DuPont as a computer programmer. Normally, engineers would turn in their programs at the end of business and they would be run by overnight operators and returned sometime the next day. However, Larrimore's results would frequently come back first thing the following morning and sometimes even that business day. While his colleagues were waiting around, Larrimore was able to be twice as productive.

He remembers, "I was asked by a couple of the engineers how I got such turnaround. I thought about it a bit and I realized I think that it came from the fact that I went over and talked to the people in the computer room. I learned that John bowled on Tuesday night so I would ask him about his bowling on Wednesday and that Mary had a kid in college and I would talk about that. While I was standing around, I would simply just talk with them as people and I think they responded to that. I hadn't thought about it at the time, but later I realized that I must be getting that kind of service because when my name came up in the queue they knew me and somebody would say, 'Why don't I run Randy's program first.'"

Too often we treat people based on perceived differences without taking the time to see our similarities. We ascribe individuals certain traits based on job position, gender, race, and ethnicity, and treat them accordingly. Businesses with traditional hierarchal structures support this divisive ideology.

However, at the end of the day, we are defined and united by far more than what can be seen on the surface. Effective leaders are able to look beyond the superficial and connect with individuals in a significant, yet often incredibly simple way. Larrimore puts treating people with dignity and respect at the top of his values list. The Golden Rule serves as a filter for his actions and decision-making in his company.

Relating to Others

Larrimore's grandfather grew up in a small Delaware town of around 8,000 people. When he was about 11 years old, his father died and he had to drop out of school to support his family. As the oldest of five children, Larrimore's grandfather took whatever position he could find to provide food for his brothers and sisters.

As he moved from job to job, he learned how to relate to people of all backgrounds. He made friends everywhere he went, impressing people with his work ethic and inviting personality. Even walking down the sidewalk in the evening, he would make a point to say hello to everyone he passed. It is this ability to connect with others that he passed on to his son, who passed it on to his son.

Larrimore remembers, "I never even realized that there were any religious differences until I got into college because my parents treated people of various religions the same. It just never crossed my mind that if you were Catholic or Jewish or something else, that it mattered. So I think this whole notion of respecting others and not really caring about their background came from my parents."

Before college, Larrimore worked during the summers at an ice plant. Most of the other employees were African-American men in their 50s who had never attended college. Even many years after Randy had left for school, every time his father would go by the plant, the workers would ask about Randy.

"Despite all I've accomplished, my father has said a number of times that one of the things he is most proud of is that when he returns to the ice plant, they ask him about his son," he says. Without a doubt, Larrimore values relating to others, just like his grandfather before him. It is a value that has shaped his personal and professional life, and guided his decision-making throughout his career.

Talking through the Tough Times

"I think that your values are always challenged, certainly at work when you are trying to make personnel decisions," Larrimore says, "We went through a restructuring where we ended up laying off a lot of people. One of the things I tried to communicate was that respecting people and having strong values doesn't mean that you can't demand performance. People get confused about that. They sometimes walk away from a discussion about treating people with respect and dignity thinking that, 'I can't fire anybody' or 'I can't be demanding from a performance sense.' My response is that it's better to communicate openly and honestly than to try to hang on to them for two or three years because you haven't been completely honest in your performance reviews."

Honesty is not always easy. Subscribing to strong values does not mean you allow inferior performance. To truly respect an individual and an organization is to strive for excellence and to make necessary changes when that level of performance is not met.

Larrimore shares, "In our restructuring, we decided in advance that we had to let people go. We did it in a way that upheld our values. We offered people the opportunity to voluntarily resign, and gave them an extra 50-percent increase in their severance benefits. It was amazing how many people really had something else they wanted to do in life. We were able to offer people protection for a period of months, which allowed them to go back to school or take time to find a new job. We ended up having two-thirds of the necessary layoffs come from voluntary resignations. The end result was that we had no legal action brought against us, not even a hint of unfairness in the way we went about our restructuring. We provided counseling; we provided outplacement services."

Effective leaders do not abandon their values in the face of adversity; they use them to guide their actions and decision-making. This perspective provides individuals and organizations with the fortitude to weather occasional setbacks, knowing that they have a foundation that everyone can believe in and count on.

Coveting Success, Not Power

Being a leader does not mean you are at the top looking down. It does not mean that you exercise control over those who work with you and wield power over them. Fear is a tool that motivates an individual to do just enough to avoid consequences. Shared success is a goal everyone will strive for.

"Unfortunately, I think the world is full of people that care more about themselves than about the company or the people within the company," Larrimore contends. "It is important for me to make high level decisions, but the company can't succeed unless the receptionist is doing her job as well. People will find me running the photocopier at night or when I am getting ready for a board meeting. At that moment, it is more important that my secretary is doing her typing, and if I have to photocopy that is fine. We do recycling around here and people catch me carrying my recycling bin and dumping it like everybody else. They seem to feel that that's odd, but it's not. Why should I ask somebody else to do it?"

Success is a by-product of everyone doing his part. No one is above or below doing what is best for the team.

Larrimore wants to build deep and meaningful two-way relationships, convey trust and respect, and express loyalty and love. These values were the ones he stressed when he selected the Dr. Seuss book to read to his employees. They guide his decisions, and in the words of Seuss, define "the places you'll go!" Adhering to core values makes you "the winning-est winner of all."

PART TWO

The Worker

Only people who take a moral approach
staying true to their convictions and
highest aspirations have careers
that are fulfilling in every way.

William Damon

Work is the opportunity to deepen and express an experience of Oneness with all beings through selfless service. While the notion of selfless service flies in the face of our normal desires and beliefs about compensation and benefits programs, it is one way to begin experiencing the true nature of God as one's own nature, purified through more and more selflessness. The intrinsic motivator – our inner nature of love – is the very nature of divinity and the very life principles behind all organisms, including organizations. Thus the big question changes from "How can we show that spiritual values can contribute to the bottom line?" to "How can we bring business into an expanded sense of our spirituality?"

Business is a learning ground for deepening our spiritual awareness. With this approach, ask yourself: "How would we conduct ourselves differently at work? How would rewards and motivations be different? How would we communicate differently? How would we work to meet our commitments to our customers? How would we deal with pollution, recycling, and 'green' issues? How would we measure the health of a company (would quarterly earnings still be important)? The answers to these questions might imply incremental or radical changes in how we operate, depending on who we are and our circumstances. The one thing I feel confident about: the answers would lead us to greater prosperity, both materially and spiritually, rather than less.

William C. Miller
Global Dharma Center.

VIII

Living Forever,
Richer and Richer

by Swami Tejomayananda

Every single being wants to live, not only live, but to live happily and forever. This is an undisputed fact, which is borne out by everything that we see around us. Even a person who commits suicide does so because he wants to end all the pain and be happy. Though we all know that we have to die one day, no one wants to die. We also want to expand and grow. Even a child watching his elder sibling wants to grow up quickly. We all want to become better in our chosen field of interest.

Let us understand the spiritual reason for this need in each of us to keep growing and to live happily forever. Vedanta says that you are *Brahman* — That thou Art — *tat tvam asi*. *Brahman* is *sat cit ānanda* (eternal, knowledge, bliss). Our nature is blissful, and therefore we cannot tolerate the presence of sorrow in life. Our nature is eternal, therefore we do not like the idea of death and mortality. Our nature is all knowing — therefore we do not tolerate ignorance. *Brahman* also means Big and Infinite. *Brahman* itself does not grow but our nature being *Brahman*, we want to grow to become Infinite.

Happiness and Money

While our true nature is *Brahman*, we also have — what seems contradictory — a natural and compelling attraction for money.

There is nothing sinful about this attraction, but it needs to be understood. The first reason for this attraction is because our daily needs and our desire for pleasure and comfort can be fulfilled only through money. If we have some passion and ambition in life — that needs money. Businessmen want to grow their industry/enterprise for which money is needed. If a person wants to become politically powerful, money is needed. One needs money if one wants to start an ashram or run a Vedanta course. Even to perform charitable work or service one needs money. Hence money is required at all levels and in every field. Therefore the attraction for money is in all of us.

The second reason for the attraction is that it is the immediate, tangible result of any work done. With that money we can buy the many material things and access to power. In itself there is nothing wrong in this attraction for money. But it becomes a problem when a person becomes very individualistic and self-centered, wanting all the wealth only for himself by whichever means, fair or foul, and does not want to spend it. There are people who have plenty of money but they cannot spend it at all, not even on themselves. The thought of spending on others gives them great pain. And there are many people who have an abundance of wealth but act like they have nothing. They live poor and die rich.

Then there are people who are only concerned about themselves or, at the most, their own family. There is nothing great about such people, because most everyone lives for themself, and this person is no different. A person who does not give to anyone else does not get any more from the Lord. But the Lord continues to give to him who gives to others. The more you give, the more you get.

Aspire for the Higher

In life, our mind is generally preoccupied with getting more and more of the same. If we get money, then we work for more money. If we have political power, we want more power and ultimately we want absolute power. Whichever field we are in, we want more and more of the same. Now, more and more of the same may add numerical value, but there will not be any inner transformation in us. We have all heard and used this expression — in the rat race, even if you win the race you still remain a rat. But if we want to become better, then we should not only aspire for more and more but must also aspire for the higher to become richer and richer.

All of us want physical comforts and money, but we must also seek greater and nobler goals. Then only we will realize the importance of higher things in life. They could be emotionally satisfying achievements or ideas that give satisfaction at intellectual level. Suppose we ask a great musician, whose material needs have been met to stop singing in exchange for a lot of money? Will he be satisfied? The musician most likely would refuse the offer and continue singing. Similarly, a sportsman is unlikely to stop playing in return for money. This shows that we are not doing things only for wealth; for there is a greater satisfaction beyond wealth that is prompting us to act and do our chosen work.

There are two ways of understanding the concept of seeking higher goals and becoming richer and richer. One is to use whatever we already have for higher and nobler purposes. Second is to seek something higher. Suppose I have talent for music, sports or some field of art. I render service to this art in such a way that more people learn and master the art. The talent is used not just for earning but for some greater purpose. Then I become richer and richer. When I sing or perform to benefit a noble cause, then my satisfaction is far greater than singing for myself. Money will come anyway. But the joy experienced is incomparable when it is dedicated to a greater cause.

Knowledge is higher than all worldly things. Among various types of knowledge, the knowledge of the Absolute Truth is the highest. Therefore, all through history and in our scriptures (*purāṇa*) all the rulers eventually renounced the world and took *saṁnyāsa* in the quest of Truth. Renunciation or sacrifice is always greater than enjoyment. A man of indulgence and self-enjoyment has never become the ideal of any nation. It is only a man of sacrifice who is respected as an ideal. That is why the Upanishad[1] says that it is only by renunciation that a person attains immortality.

If Rama, in the *Rāmāyaṇa*, had by force hung on to his kingdom and refused to go to the forest, he would not have become Rama, the ideal person; worshipped and revered through generations. Bharata, though he got the kingdom, sacrificed it and that is why he became great. In this renunciation there is gain of the highest Truth there is no loss at all.

The Highest Gain

What is the true gain in life? In the *Bhagavad Gītā*, there is a beautiful verse, which says that the attainment of Self-knowledge is that having gained which the person does not consider any other gain greater. Here "having gained which" are the important words. At a given time, when a person desires something, he may not consider any other gain greater than fulfilling that one desire. When we desire for something we do not have, fulfilling that desire may appear to be the greatest gain. But as soon as that desire is fulfilled that gain does not seem to the biggest gain after all because another strong desire has arisen in the heart. What is significant is the state of mind after the object of desire has been attained.

When a child asks for a toy, the child promises not to ask for anything again but can only keep the promise as long as he gets the toy. The moment he gets it and breaks it, he wants something more. But the *Bhagavad Gītā* speaks about the Highest Gain — having gained which man does not seek anything greater than that.

In the world when we gain something, we can also lose it. Our gain is subject to loss. Even when a poor man becomes a rich man, he loses something — the joy that he had when he was a poor man. The greatest joy was that no one came to him for donation! Further, as a poor man he could sit under a tree or go wherever he wanted. As a rich man, he cannot do any of that. Poverty has its own joy and gains. The worldly gain is always associated with loss of something in exchange and secondly, what one gains is subject to being lost someday.

But the gain of spiritual knowledge of our own Self, which is infinite and blissful, is such that it will never get lost. I can lose something other than myself but I cannot lose myself. That is always with me once I know it. And in that gain, I will not lose anything else. In that joy and happiness everything is already included. That's why the *Bhagavad Gītā* says that the person established in the Highest Truth is not shaken even by huge mountain-like sorrow. A true renunciate (*saṁnyāsī*) does not lose anything or have the fear of losing anything.

Growth Through Knowledge

As we continue to use what we have for a higher and higher purpose, and at the same time continue to seek what is higher and higher, we will find that the pursuit of knowledge is wonderful; and in that the knowledge of the Absolute is the highest. Our nature is consciousness, blissful, and infinite. And that's why we are not satisfied with little things. We want to grow continuously and this is possible only through knowledge.

We can be infinite by either becoming nothing or by becoming everything. That's the most important thing to know. We all want to become somebody in life. Either we should become everybody or we should become nobody. The path of total surrender, called *bhakti mārga* in Hindu scriptures, is where a devotee says, "I am nothing, Oh Lord! You are the only one." In the path of knowledge the person says, "That infinite truth cannot be different from me. It is my own Self." He sees that Self in everyone, this way that person becomes the richest! He continues to expand yet at the same time there is no attachment to anything. So, totally contented in the Self, for such a person everything grows, including material gain and that person continues to live forever, richer and richer. Even after his death, the name of the person remains a source of inspiration for countless years. Not only does he become rich, he also enriches everyone else's life.

There are two types of famous men. One is like Ravana,

who, wanting to grow himself, pulls everyone down. The other type is like Rama. His greatness was that he made every tiny creature great — including the monkeys. Everyone reveres this kind of person. As Saint Tulsidas says in *Rāmacarita Mānasa* that Lord Rama's greatness was such that he raised even the likes of monkeys, who jump from one tree to another, to the level of divinity.

Thus a truly great person is one, who is not only great himself, but who also raises every small being to the level of greatness. And such a person lives forever, richer and richer. The person who wants to grow at the expense of making everyone small is hated by all around him, and can never become a source of inspiration.

This simple secret of living forever is the most beautiful topic of spirituality. What is spirituality? Spirituality does not lie in any particular action. It lies in being who you are. It is being and remaining rooted in that Being. Then whatever you do becomes spirituality. So what is this being and doing?

The Vision of Oneness

Suppose someone says that he is a singer. We can ask him to sing and he can demonstrate that he is a singer. Similarly, if he is a *yogī* and knows *yoga āsana*, we can ask him to perform. But if we hear that someone is an honest man, can we ask him to show some honesty to us? Is honesty an action? But if that person is really honest, that honesty will be there in all actions — in what he thinks, feels, and does. If a person is a very kind person, then everything he does, speaks, or thinks is kind. In the same way, if a person is spiritual, then everything about him is spiritual. Spirituality is the vision of the oneness of all beings — that you are one with all there is, and no one is different from you or separate from you. When you begin to feel that oneness with all, then you become more and more spiritual. You learn to look at your life as a whole and you live a whole life. You do not fragment, you do not go on dividing your life — this is my personal life, this is my public life. There are no such divisions.

It is only one life and you are the same in all. When a person feels oneness, then he cannot cheat anyone because he will be cheating himself! That vision of oneness is called spiritual vision and when you have that, then you live forever and richer and richer.

FOOTNOTE:

1   *samnāysa sūkta, mahā-nārāyaṇopaniṣad* 4:12.

IX

Behaving Spiritually in the Workplace

by C. Diane Ealy

Our spirituality arises from love, unconditional love. I have to add that phrase because we have generally done such a poor job of understanding the true nature of love. All love is unconditional. If we give or get the message, "I will love you if ..." then there are strings attached and it's not love. It might be jealousy, greed, fear, control, or some other emotion or need, but it's not love.

At its least complicated, spirituality is love. Love gives us a larger view of events and enables us to be accepting and non-judgmental, perspectives that are a necessity in a healthy workplace. Your personal relationship with love extended into the external world forms the basis for your spiritual response. An important point to remember is that we can love others without feeling the need or desire to have sex with them. I want to emphasize this understanding as we have more discussions focused on expressing our spirituality through love in the workplace.

Spirit Caution

You don't have to love or even like other people to be spiritually responsive. Your focus is on your inner experience of love for yourself arising from your loving spiritual part — your Self. This is not a narcissistic focus with deeply held self-doubt at its core, but rather an all-encompassing, non-judgmental spiritually derived love. This is your Self.

Love and Fear

Staying attuned to your spirituality means staying aligned with love and being willing to manifest that connection through your behavior. The emotion that is most likely to pull you away from an inner experience of love is fear. Many psychologists believe that humans have two basic emotions, love and fear, and that all other emotions arise from these two. While attempts to prove or disprove this idea continue, let us assume that this idea is correct.

Spirit Tip

Fear-based emotions disconnect you from your spirituality. They include anger, frustration, grief, jealousy, insecurity, sadness, and greed. Behaviorally, their manifestations are as distinct as we are and involve yelling, sarcasm, cynicism, shutting down, put-downs, deceit, conceit, and dismissing another's ideas or feelings. When these behaviors happen in the workplace, efficiency and productivity take a major hit.

The love/fear perspective gives us a different way of looking at our reactions to other people and circumstances that can help us be more in-charge of our spiritual responsiveness. And it can provide us with insight into others' behaviors as well. If love and fear are our two basic emotions, then all other emotions are derived from one of these two. Only by understanding the basis for emotions that pull us away from our spirituality can we learn how to stay on track in becoming a more spiritual person.

Simplifying Fear

Love-based responses are easy to pick out — joy, kindness, compassion, happiness, and gratitude, for example. Fear-based emotions can be a bit trickier to explain. How can anger, jealousy, frustration, or greed have their roots in fear? Discovering the answer to that question involves the proverbial peeling away of layers.

Think about the last time something at work made you angry. Perhaps it was a co-worker's or boss's behavior, or an action taken by the company itself. The question to ask yourself about that anger is —What was I afraid of when I reacted with anger? Some common fears underlying workplace anger are loss of control, being controlled, fear of losing your job, fear of appearing incompetent, fear of loss, or even fear of getting too close to another person — fear of intimacy either professional or personal. You can apply the same question to other emotions to see what you come up with in terms of their fear connections. In *The Alchemy of Fear*, author Kay Gilley estimates that 90 percent of workplace behavior is fear-based.

As we explore common situations that happen to most of us while on the job, we will look for the probable association between the fear and the behavior. Once you understand the fear that is actually being expressed, reconnecting with your inner sense of love so you can respond spiritually is much easier. Naming the fear takes its power away, giving it back to you, where that power belongs. So the more aware you are of what triggers you into fear-based reactions, the quicker you can acknowledge the feeling, take action, if appropriate, then move back to love and spirituality.

Spirit Guide

Our culture gives us lots of negative ideas about expressing fear. Complete the following sentences to clarify the messages you have picked up:

*Fear is*_____

*Fear is*_____

*Fear is*_____

*Fear is*_____

The question often arises as to why we would feel anger or frustration instead of fear, if fear is, indeed, the true source of the feeling. Our culture gives us the message that fear equals weakness. Only sissies are afraid. Most of us learn very early to transform fear into a more acceptable feeling such as anger, frustration, or sadness and depression, among others. Typically, little boys quickly learn that anger is acceptable while girls learn that sadness or depression is okay. In our attempt to appear strong or at least to conform to others' expectations of what our behavior should be, we learn to hide the truth from ourselves as well as others.

As long as we don't know what is really going on inside ourselves, we will be at the mercy of our emotional reactions rather than being in charge of our responses. When we begin to be aware of and acknowledge our feelings, we give ourselves more options for our behavior. We strengthen our chances of behaving spiritually.

Spirit Wisdom

If you begin discussing your fears with others, they may become uncomfortable. What you end up doing, inadvertently, is acting as a mirror, reflecting their fears back to them. Once this dynamic happens, they have to face their fears just as you are doing. Even without open discussions, your new behaviors arising from your spiritual connection will be noticed. Some people will welcome these changes while others will be unsettled. You may find yourself pulling away from people you had previously been close to. I know I'm on the right track in my spiritual growth when these types of people say to me, "Diane, you used to be so nice."

Getting a Grip on Fear

I'd like you to pause for a moment and think about what can happen in your workplace that makes you angry, frustrated, anxious, or triggers any other non-spiritual reaction. A recurring situation may come to mind, such as a weekly meeting. Perhaps you think of a particular person and his or her behavior or general attitude. Now describe this event or person in writing. This act gives you a different perspective by externalizing the memory and helps in gaining objectivity. Next, complete the following steps:

1. Note your feelings about the situation.

2. Ask yourself — What fear might be the basis for these feelings?
3. Name or briefly describe the fear itself.

By taking these steps, you are honoring and acknowledging your original feelings and providing yourself with the means and understanding of shifting your reaction to a more positive one.

At times, you may not be able to figure out exactly which fear has been hooked. Simply acknowledging the existence of fear can be enough to enable you to let it go so you can realign yourself with your spirituality. Then the next time you encounter that particular person or situation, you can remind yourself of what feelings usually get set off in this circumstance, stopping the unwanted, negative reaction, and engaging in a spiritual response by consciously shifting yourself into love.

Real Life

It works like this. Suppose you have a co-worker, Jack, who is irritating to you because you consider his work substandard. You have no authority over Jack, but you do have to associate with him. He also likes to complain a lot about being busy and the more he complains, the more you find yourself becoming disgusted and frustrated with him. You have noticed that when you have to work with Jack, you feel angry toward your supervisor for failing to take action to either improve Jack's work or to fire him. So you have identified irritation, disgust, frustration, and anger in connection with this co-worker. Clearly, you're not responding spiritually to Jack!

To move forward in this situation, you first have to accept that someone else cannot make you feel a particular way — you are in charge of your responses. A person may trigger certain emotional reactions within you, but what you do with your inner feelings is your choice. Let's stay away from whether or not you are justified in reacting negatively to Jack; that would take us into a head-trip and divert us from our spiritual path. Your reaction is what it is and you have the power to change that reaction to a response.

Spirit Tip

Try these suggestions when conducting an inner exploration into the root of your feelings. Sometimes people find it scary to explore their feelings. Keep breathing. Cutting off your breath is one sure sign that you're moving into fear. Write things down to gain objectivity. Approach the activity as a treasure hunt. After all, you hold a myriad of undiscovered treasures within.

Now that you have identified your feelings toward Jack, ask yourself what fears might be underlying them. You may have to play with the wording of the question to help you approach the fears from different perspectives. Exploring the possibilities with an open mind always helps. Again, writing all of this information down aids in keeping it manageable. Try the following questions:

- When I am irritated (or frustrated or angry) with Jack, what fear might be set off?
- What are some of my major fears around work and being employed by this company?
- How does this co-worker's behavior tap into my fears?
- Finally, there's the therapist's trick question: If I knew what fears were beneath my feelings toward this individual, what would those fears be?

With the answers to these questions, you're ready to label your fears. If you have given this part of the process adequate attention and still can't uncover the exact fear, don't get bogged down. Trust that somewhere in your psyche you know. Move forward. The answer often presents itself later.

You might discover that all four feelings are tapping into a fear that you are wasting your time and efforts with this organization. You fear that your work standards will never be appreciated and rewarded by a boss or company that accepts substandard work from someone else. If this assumption is true, you are wasting your time and ought to be looking for another job. But a job search is often loaded with fear. And you selected this company when you first took the job, so you might be afraid that you will make the same mistake if you try for another job with a different organization. Whew!

Fears often snowball like this one irrational thought connected to another — and it's a lot easier to become angry or frustrated than it is to face those fears. Soon you are feeling overwhelmed and a long way from being spiritual. How do you find your way out?

Taking Your Power Back

Writing down this trail of fears helps in understanding their irrationality and gives you some distance from them. Now you're ready to shift internally into being aligned with your spiritual self. From this positive perspective you can continue looking at your fears by asking yourself some more questions. Is my fear of not being appreciated grounded in reality? Does my boss compliment me on my work or do things that let me know he appreciates my efforts? Do I accept these compliments or do I dismiss them? What kinds of people does this organization promote and do I really care? Do I want a promotion or am I happy staying at my current position?

Lastly, ask yourself — What do my fears do for me? This question is often the hardest to answer. We don't like to think that any negative behaviors have benefits for us. Yet they do or we wouldn't engage in them. Some people who shift fear into anger get energized from that anger. It helps them feel justified in other negative behaviors like complaining or causing chaos that they can then "fix." Once we understand what our fears are doing for us, then we can begin exploring how to have those needs met using more constructive behaviors.

Spirit Tip

The fears we're talking about aren't the warnings about physical danger, such as don't walk down a dark alley. We're focusing on the fears that arise during your interactions with others. These are the feelings that have their origins

*in deep-seated beliefs around your vulnerabilities that may
or may not have any basis in reality. These fears keep you
disconnected from your spirituality.*

One thing that becomes apparent as a result of this self-examination is that your irritation with Jack's work style has given you the opportunity to face and clear out your own fears. How do Jack's work habits affect you now? This exercise isn't about getting to the place of liking Jack or the quality of his work. It's about lowering your stress level and increasing your work enjoyment by responding spiritually to this situation.

Reaping the Benefits

Now that you know what fears are being set off by Jack's work habits, you can focus your attention on facing those fears. Once you do this, you will likely be unaffected by Jack. Or if you have to work closely with him on some project, you will deal directly with the quality of his work and avoid becoming enmeshed in internal reactions that are inappropriate and unproductive. In other words, you can speak to him openly about his need to improve his work without feeling angry. Or you may decide that bringing in your supervisor to help Jack improve his work is more appropriate. Or you may request that you and Jack not be assigned to the same projects.

From a spiritual perspective that is free of fear-based emotions, you will decide the most constructive course of action. Whatever you do, your focus is on integrating your psyche rather than on attacking Jack and making him the bad guy. Your commitment to your well-being lies at the core of your spiritual responsiveness.

The key to this entire process is your ability to align yourself internally with a sense of unconditional love and, simultaneously, with your spirituality. This connection provides you with a calmness that allows you to have far more choices of how you want to respond to a situation than does being fearful. Inner peace is the source of "saying the right thing at the right time," of making healthy decisions for yourself and acting on them, of getting out of and staying away from abusive workplace people and situations. While we are often taught that anger is strong and love is weak, just the opposite is true. Love is the most powerful feeling we possess and if we allow it, it will take very good care of us.

X

The Worship of Laziness
by Swami Jyotirmayananda

Laziness is the very embodiment of evil for an individual as well as for society. It is considered one of the worst enemies of spiritual progress. In Sanskrit it is called *ālasya,* and it is an effect of *tamas* or inertia. Being a highly contagious disease, it enters into the human personality in a very subtle manner. Whenever you encounter a lazy person, you, too, tend to become lazy.

If you study laziness in relation to the individual, to society and to the whole concept of progress and material pursuit, you will be amazed how hard people work just to adore the Goddess of Laziness. If you walk into a busy office where many people are working, you will find they are working hard from morning until evening so they can finish their work, go home and be lazy. People work in order not to work. They plan their entire lives around the ultimate goal of constantly sitting in an easy chair and watching the sunset in a place like Miami Beach.

Since people do not really understand laziness, they think it is an ideal to aspire for. People spend a lot of money acquiring many possessions in order to become lazy. Many feel that when they have no work at hand, no pressing responsibilities, no use for mental or physical energy, they will be in a better position. But that is a ghastly idea for people who really think. Those who don't think aspire for a life of inactivity, and this concept has become the bane of present civilization.

Laziness operates in a very subtle manner. The moment you feel comfortable, you begin to feel there is no harm if you do your work tomorrow. You have worked for so many years. When will you enjoy life? When will you take that well-deserved vacation for thirty days? When you become too indulgent in that type of thought, you begin to adore laziness. If this happens, your mind constantly develops a conflict towards the set up of work in which you are placed and the present state of affairs.

Laziness leads to a weak will, which in turn leads to a sick mind. A sick mind, in turn, generates numerous evils such as anger, hatred, and greed, and life gradually becomes more and more bitter. Therefore, if you know how *māyā* operates by creating laziness, you will not allow yourself to be tricked by her.

Laziness has two important expressions — physical and mental. Physical laziness expresses itself in the form of increasing boredom and a tendency to become physically inactive and unbalanced. Mental laziness implies the development of a wrong philosophy or attitude towards life, which gives rise to expressions of the lower self. You may read volumes of books, yet if you are mentally lazy, you cannot be an inspiring or healthy thinker.

If you were to study the life of philosophers and their philosophies, you will find that those who did not integrate their personalities through dynamic service of humanity, and who confined their studies to libraries and concrete walls, evolve sickly philosophies. It is tiring to read their works, and after having studied them you simply become exhausted; no inspiration is gained. On the other hand, there are people like Ramakrishna and other great Sages and Saints, who are not such erudite philosophers, but who have spent their lives doing dynamic service for humanity. They have spent less time with books and more time with intensive living in daily life. Their thoughts were so dynamic that today they still continue to rule the masses through creative inspiration.

It is important to understand the evil of laziness and the

psychology behind it. The mistaken idea that happiness and comfort will come when you have no responsibility or work is what makes you inclined to laziness. For example, as people age, each birthday reminds them that they are aging, and in turn they begin to suggest to themselves, "What have I gained? I am still working hard liked a laborer! Am I to go on doing this for the rest of my life? This is for those who are young, not for me." So they gradually try to retire from activity and develop the concept that to be successful, dignified and honorable, they should simply give orders to others and do nothing at all themselves. But then they gradually develop internal frustration because inertia is not the law of life. Inertia opposes life, and so they find themselves slipping more and more into mental complexes. And if this is not bad enough, people outside them interpret this dullness and laziness as fortunate. They are actually jealous of the miseries of others. If you are jealous of such lazy people, it is out of ignorance.

Having looked into the fallacy of laziness, you must wage war against it. Since you understand that laziness is not to be desired, then work actively until old age. Never present before yourself the idea that you should work hard now so that you can retire early. Rather, constantly hold the idea that you should work every day, with a balanced effort, both mentally and physically. Physical work should not be ignored. It does not matter if your hands become rough and your limbs strained; it is much better to keep your body and mind working and active than to be running after luxury. Luxury and laziness are brothers. People who have acquired many luxuries have also acquired many involvements with possessions, wealth and empty achievements. They are constantly restless.

Hatha Yoga exercises will remove inertia of the body, but the deeper or subtler roots of inertia are removed only when you start making your whole personality useful to humanity. Such is the law. For example, suppose you are a householder and also a good instructor of some subject. Every day you teach your children. But you have another possibility — to invite from your neighboring area many children and teach them the same subject. Now you have started a school where fifty students come. Your own children are also included, and so you find that with the same amount of effort you are performing a more purposeful action. And as a result, you develop more inspiration and energy within yourself.

Removing Laziness

In order to remove laziness it is important that your actions be purposeful. So, apart from doing Yoga exercises and *prāṇāya-ma* (breathing exercises to energize your body with vitality), there must be a purposeful plan in which your body is utilized. Therefore, an aspirant should welcome manual labor or physical exertion. He should not run away from physical work, but rather plan to work physically according to his capacity.

An important aspect of physical activity is working in the open. Many people think such work is useless, but they are unaware that nature can cure many ailments. People who remain lazy ultimately have to go into areas where they can be more exposed to nature. So it makes sense to plan a life in a way that you work and dig in the earth, take care of the trees, bend up and down, move in the sun and the rain, and expose yourself to the weather. You may become a little rusty, but it is much better to possess an enduring body, vigorous health and good appetite than to become a weakling and a prey to constant disharmony.

Healthy physical work is an important basis for spiritual advancement. By doing such work day by day you accomplish something that satisfies your mind and, at the same time, opens up greater possibilities for mental advancement. When your body is healthy your mind becomes more alert. It will not suggest to you that you are getting older, but will suggest to you that, with a basis of many positive experiences from the past, you are becoming brighter and more mature.

If your physical body tends towards laziness, you impose upon your mind an erroneous way of thinking. You feel that since you are aging, you are becoming weak and should let others do the strenuous type of work. You may even begin to justify traits like forgetfulness, inactivity and procrastination, and actually feel that they are something to be proud of. You have done all that you wanted to do, and since now you are prosperous and wealthy, why should you comply with the general laws of decorum and life?

In order to overcome laziness, every action should be performed with intense interest. Your whole heart and soul should go into it. You should not try to rush through something because you feel you have something more interesting waiting ... such as delicious smelling food that you can't wait to get to! The truth is you cannot really delight in food if you have not given proper exercise to your body. You will simply develop indigestion. Similarly, if you have not achieved harmony through proper exercise of your body in your daily life, then when evening comes you cannot enjoy real sleep. Those who overcome laziness sleep soundly. The joys of a sound sleep, active body and healthy life are beyond the reach of people who live an abnormal life. Those joys are greater than all the treasures of the world.

If a particular kind of work tires you, then bring variation into it. Adjust your personality in such a way that if a task requires more thoughtfulness, you should be able to exercise your thought and perform the work effectively. If work requires more manual labor, then also you should have a mental attitude that every act of labor is in harmony with your spiritual evolution. Every brick you pick up, every thorn you remove, all paperwork done to promote order, helps you.

Don't look around to see if anyone is watching you work. Even if nobody sees you do it, you have contributed to a process of internal purification and your action becomes *karma yoga*. Since you are keeping yourself busy, your mind becomes brighter and brighter. The knowledge of the scriptures flows into your mind automatically, without going through voluminous studies. A bright and joyous mind spontaneously comprehends the secrets and profound realities of life.

Another method of overcoming laziness involves the practice of surrender to God in your daily life. Your mind must be accustomed to the positive vibrations of *nāma japa,* the repetition of Divine Name. There is a saying in Hindi, "*mukh me Ram hāth me kām*" — "Keep Rama on your tongue and let your hands be involved in action." Your life must become a continuous process of *nāma japa,* implying a constant affirmation of the fact that you are in touch with the Divine Self. You must be constantly aware that there is the Divine Hand behind every work you do.

Therefore, with deep thoughtfulness and sincere devotion, perform a work. If you have performed it well, you will not expect any reward, because that performance itself will give you great joy. You gradually become detached from all activity. It doesn't matter how the reward will come, because once the work is over you become completely detached. When activity is continuous you become increasingly dynamic, though detached, and you begin to enjoy internal peace and mental alertness. When there is mental alertness, all great qualities express in your life. You do not procrastinate, you become more qualitative, and you become brief but dynamic in your expression.

In Hindu mysticism, Goddess Saraswati removes laziness. On the other hand, if you are lazy, you are offending Her. Goddess Saraswati is the Goddess of expression, and if you are lazy, you lack expression in your body, mind and thought.

Laziness is also offensive to Goddess Lakshmi, because where there is laziness, there is constant sighing, grieving, quarreling — and these things are like the croaking of toads to the ears of Goddess Lakshmi. Laziness is also offensive to Goddess Durga, who is intent upon removing negative qualities from those who are sincere. And once the Goddess has removed all the negative qualities from the sincere aspirant, She dumps them all on the lazy person.

If the ideal of dynamic and purposeful activity throughout life could be imbibed by society, many of its ills would be easily remedied. The social structure should not be based on the worship of the Goddess of Laziness, but on the worship of great Hanuman, the vibrant embodiment of energy, power and action. If this were so, automatically there would be less evil. People who work sincerely are joyous; they do not harbor constant anger, hatred, disharmony or internal conflict.

Therefore, by utilizing your energy day by day, and by taking recourse to vigilance, *satsaṅga,* and a rhythmic pattern of active life, you can effectively fight laziness. And once laziness is removed, your life flows like a sparkling river to the Ocean of Universal Life.

XI

The Challenge of Action

by Swami Chinmayananda

[*The following is taken from a talk given by Swami Chinmayananda in the early 1980s.*]

Life consists of meeting challenges. When one has stopped meeting challenges and responding to them, that organism is dead. If a plant stops reacting to water and does not give out new buds, if a bird does not chirp or a dog does not bark, they do not respond to external stimuli and are considered to be dead. From birth to death, in every moment of our existence, we are responding to external stimuli. We act constantly, because action is the insignia of life in us. While thus acting, we face many inner and outer challenges from our spouses, children, neighbors, society, and ourselves. Every moment, every individual has to meet them alone, without anyone's help.

When a child is born, it knows nothing. After some time the sense organs begin to function and he starts learning from others. As he matures he becomes educated and specializes in a field of his choice, gathering information from other people regarding their experiences. This indirect knowledge — gathered from books, journals, discussions, and lectures — is preserved in the memory and is called proficiency. It is this knowledge of proficiency that we use to express ourselves in the world. When compared with other nations proficiency is very high in India. This is because right from childhood, we are taught many subjects. By the time we graduate, a vast amount of knowledge has been gained. Yet, in spite of this proficiency and availability of machinery and raw materials, the country is poor. Why? Unfortunately we do not investigate this contradiction scientifically but take shelter behind words such as "luck" or "destiny." We use excuses such as "I am not blessed, I am an unlucky person." We even go to the extent of blaming the stars and planets for not being in their right places, thereby causing our failures.

The rishis of Vedic times were subjective scientists who analyzed life itself; they were not content with merely finding an excuse. They thought over the paradox in a scientific manner and came to the conclusion that success in life does not depend on proficiency alone but on efficiency. We may have all the knowledge and be proficient, but if this knowledge cannot be used efficiently, we cannot succeed in our endeavors. According to the rishis, the proficiency that a person has in his understanding must flow through him and express itself through work in such a manner that the end result has an extra glow — an added beauty. This glow, beauty, and perfection in the job done are the measures of the efficiency of the man.

Efficiency is not dependent on external factors such as clothes or hairstyle, but lies in the extra dynamism and beauty that surrounds a given piece of work. I may be proficient in many things, but if at the appropriate time it is not available, it is like a stay order from the court. I have inherited my father's money, but the account is frozen until the court disposes off all other claims against it. A student who is well prepared sometimes finds that his mind has gone totally blank in the examination hall, whereas all his knowledge comes flooding back into memory the moment he steps out.

The Key to Efficiency

On further analysis, the rishis discovered that in order for one's knowledge to emerge readily through the fingertips, it has to pass through highly sophisticated equipment called the mind. The key to efficiency is therefore the condition of the mind. If the mind is disturbed or agitated, the flow of knowledge becomes blocked. If, however, the mind can be trained to remain calm, serene, alert and vigilant under all circumstances, one's knowledge can be easily utilized. This leads to spectacular success. When the mind is properly attuned, performance in the outside world is bound to be excellent. Excellent performances can only lead to excellent results.

Thus success or failure is not a matter of luck. It is a question of adjustment of the inner equipment. But the rishis did not stop with merely finding that the mind must be controlled if one is to succeed in life. They wanted to find out ways and means of keeping the mind quiet. They discovered that the mind remains agitated until it finds an altar at which it can pour out its dedication and love. Therefore, the secret of efficiency is to discover a goal, a purpose in life. The goal need not necessarily be religious; it can be professional or political. All great men of achievement, who have left their mark upon the world, were able to achieve great things because they had a steady vision of the goal to be reached. And having fixed the goal, they continued to work toward achieving it after surrendering all confusions worries and anxieties at the altar of their chosen goal. It is through adhering to a goal that we master the art of translating our proficiency in whatever we are doing. Then we are able to overcome all obstacles and become established in our task or profession.

When thus we achieve success, it becomes our duty to serve society. Why service? Because the whole society — the entire universe — is one integral whole. Every one of us is, as it were, a cell in one body of which we are all a part. And everyone is as important as everyone else. To serve others is to recognize the Oneness of the universe — the cosmic form of the Lord (*virāṭ rūpa*). All of us are part of One great individual entity, the One total integral body. Once this is understood, your joy becomes my joy; your misery becomes my misery. When this greater vision of Oneness of the world has entered our minds, there is an involvement in life — a concern for other living beings. We develop a feeling that we are not just serving someone else; we are serving ourselves.

The efficiency of a person is found expressed in the dynamism of his actions, and in his cheerfulness at his work. One who has this secret power in him, to him is all success and achievement. In fact, an efficient man's work really endures and continues, yielding a growing dividend of joy and cheer to himself, and brings an unrolling light, grace, and blessings to the society. An artist working in a studio, a poet singing his poems, a sculptor at his marble-lump, a surgeon in the operation-theatre ... why, everyone from the greatest leaders of men to the simplest farmers on the field, when they are inspired by the work they are doing, they exhibit an efficiency which is almost divine. To the extent they are inspired, their work also becomes enduring and a continuous blessing to mankind.

Swami Chinmayananda

XII

The Transformation of Work
by Lewis Richmond

One of Buddhism's key contributions is its teaching that most human suffering and injustice has its origins in desire — desire for wealth, power, security, safety, and long life. We are all, to one degree or another, prisoners of such desires. That is our human nature, and commerce is simply the collective expression of all those individual wants and needs. Whether we want a loaf of bread, a thinner nose, a faster car, an education for our child, a medicine for our pain, or an evening at a Rolling Stones concert, there is a commercial transaction that can satisfy that want.

But desires are not all equivalent. Though the desire for a loaf of bread is not the same as the desire for a Rolex watch — either materially or spiritually — our consumer society is based on the premise that it is, that any human desire worth having is worth fulfilling. The advertising industry exists primarily to stimulate these desires and in some cases to invent them out of whole cloth. Such a marketplace does not ask questions or make value judgments. Instead, it assumes that the best way to satisfy the most people is to let them all freely pursue their own self-interest. Even where the legal system draws the line — with illegal drugs, for example — that line is rather arbitrary. Nicotine is as addictive as heroin and arguably as harmful.

It has been left to spiritual leaders, such as the Buddha, to challenge our fundamental assumptions about human desire. Though known to posterity as a great spiritual teacher, the

Buddha was, until the age of twenty-nine, the ancient equivalent of a billionaire, a prince of wealth and privilege. His spiritual awakening began when he realized that all his wealth and power could not provide him with true happiness. He took to traveling in disguise among the common people, where he experienced firsthand the suffering of the people whose labor was the basis of his own wealth. Shortly after that, he left the palace forever and became a wandering monk. The Buddha's core message is that human nature is not fixed. Unlike Thomas Hobbes, Adam Smith, and other Western thinkers who accepted human nature as a given and whose philosophies form the basis of modern commerce, the Buddha felt that our human nature is capable of transformation or, to be more precise, self-transformation.

If that is true, then the free market is even freer than we usually think. Suppose everyone suddenly became convinced that Rolex watches caused heart attacks. The market for Rolex watches would collapse overnight. People would throw away their old ones, nobody would buy new ones, and soon the makers of Rolex watches would be out of business. This is not just a fantasy. Such things do happen. For example, the great "Alar" scare in 1989 convinced consumers that apples contained a dangerous pesticide. Apple prices fell precipitously. Some apple farms nearly failed. It turned out that the scare was a false alarm, and the apples were not dangerous. But it was too late for some small farmers.

Emphasizing Spiritual Values

The marketplace begins in the mind.

To put it another way: The marketplace does not control us, we control the marketplace — at least to the extent that our inner values and character are stronger than the lure of advertisements and possessions. If we truly want our system of commerce and the conditions of our employment to change, then the place to start is with ourselves. The sum total of what each of us must have or can do without creates the whole economy that employs us and sustains us. If we built an economic system based more on loaves of bread and less on Rolex watches, more on compassion than on competition, more on spiritual than material values, we might end up with a very different world from the one we live in today. The contemporary Vietnamese Buddhist teacher Thich Nhat Hanh once said that if every American were to forgo one alcoholic drink and one serving of meat per week, it would feed the population of his native country for a year. What would induce us Americans to do that? Why is fasting such a common spiritual practice throughout the world? Is it because it helps to remember what is really important? The ultimate solution to the inequities and failings of free-market capitalism is not economic but spiritual. In the end, it is our own deeply held beliefs and values that create the world in which we all are fated to live.

If an emphasis on spiritual values becomes sufficiently strong among a large enough group of people, the marketplace will begin to reflect that desire. There are already some markets that are almost entirely the creation of such a shift in values, such as the organic food industry or alternative healthcare. Even meditation centers and corporate mindfulness programs are filling a market need. And what about the workplace itself? Employment operates like any other market, according to the laws of supply and demand. Right now, for example, there is a worldwide shortage of computer programmers, which accounts for their premium starting salaries and benefits. But remember the old slogan, "Suppose they gave a war and nobody came." Suppose money was no longer the prime attraction for talented, spiritually aware job seekers. My workshops are full of people for whom the lure of riches no longer suffices. For them, quality of work and quality of life are what count. And that reflects a larger trend. One research institute estimates that over the next ten years 25 percent of Americans will become "downshifters," and strive to scale their life back to some degree.

There was a time when the workweek was six days, when health benefits, flex time, maternity leave, and the host of other workplace benefits we now take for granted did not exist. Seventy-five years ago, a worker who insisted on such perquisites would have been laughed out of the boss's office and probably fired. Many business executives would argue that catering to workers' spiritual needs is going too far. I read recently of one chief executive of a midwestern firm who complained to his human resources staff about fuzzyheaded, "New Age" ideas among some middle managers. "I want you to develop a test to identify those people," he grumbled, "so we can get rid of them." I'd be willing to bet that "those people" were that firm's most talented managers.

On the other hand, some progressive companies are establishing wellness programs, yoga classes, meditation and prayer rooms, and on-site health clubs. There are now corporate training programs in mindfulness, and Buddhist meditation teachers are being recruited to lead them. Companies usually need robust earnings to support such perks, and in all likelihood such programs will be the first to be cut when profits dip. The fact that these programs exist at all is a good first step, but they are not necessarily a sign-yet-of fundamental change in the core business culture.

True Happiness

How many of us in business stop to ask ourselves: Why are we doing all this? What, ultimately, is the point? What is profit, really, and why is it important? All of this worldwide commercial activity is, at the end of the day, supposed to be contributing to human happiness, to contentment, to a better life for people. Otherwise, why do it? And is it really providing more happiness to more people? The vast, interconnected global economy that we have created presumably exists to satisfy at least some of these goals. Or does it? Do we control it, or does it control us? Does it exist for the benefit of everyone or only the powerful few?

And if happiness is the ultimate goal, then what is happiness, anyway? Is it just having more money in the bank? More cars in the garage, more vacation homes? Most people would agree that happiness, at root, is a spiritual, not material, value. That is what Jesus and the Buddha taught, what all great spiritual leaders taught.

But why seek to be happy? Why make a living? Why live at all?

The philosopher Albert Camus began his masterpiece *The Myth of Sisyphus* by writing, "Judging whether or not life is worth living amounts to answering the fundamental question of all philosophy." Each of us, whether we realize it or not, asks ourselves that question every day, and every day we make that judgment anew in favor of life. We do want to keep on living, against all odds. We even find joy in it, wherever we can.

Is it possible to imagine a world where we can expect to make more than a living, to find not just necessity in our work but joy as well? Can that be the next entitlement for workers of the twenty-first century? If that seems too much to ask, I would argue, why ask for less? That said, such a change in fundamental values and outlook will not happen quickly. It may take ten, twenty, fifty, or a hundred years. Many people in the developing world are just emerging from grinding poverty — just as Europe was a few hundred years ago. And even in the United States, the richest country on the planet, there is much poverty. People in the world's emerging nations may need to have their three televisions and two cars long enough to assure themselves that such luxuries are not the be all and end all of human existence, as the American TV channels they receive on their satellite dishes would have them believe. The Buddha himself needed twenty-nine years of the princely life before he came to that same conclusion, and he was a born sage! Materialism as the reigning creed of human existence may need to complete its life cycle just as previous belief systems have done. But in the end, it is not our worldly desires that will set the grand agenda for our long-term future as a species but our spiritual aspirations.

It is to that end that I have written this book [the author's *Work As a Spiritual Practice*] and it is in the service of that goal that I encourage you to believe in yourself, to trust yourself, and to demand the best of yourself and your workplace. When we believe that the world makes us, that it determines what we can and cannot do, then we see ourselves as small and weak. But when we understand that we make the world — individually and together then we become formidable and strong. The light that radiates out from the whole of the Jewel Net is the sum of each of its six billion diamonds. That starry sky, in which you and I shine as brightly as any sun, is our only home.

XIII

Dynamism: A Combination of Vision and Action

by Swami Tejomayananda

It is worth observing that all great religious movements sprang only from meditation and contemplation. The spiritual teachings from all the great masters originated from that quietude and contemplation. In the course of time, many rituals, activities, customs and traditions sprang up, and the original message of knowledge became completely lost. That is why in most temples nowadays we find everything except devotion to God, and in the educational institutions we find all kind of faculties, except love for knowledge.

Meaningless activities without the foundation of a vision, or knowledge and understanding of the purpose, can only lead to feverish activity. This leads to stress, and we feel the need to attend various seminars on how to lead a stress-free life. Yet the people who organize the workshops are themselves under stress because they want the seminar to be successful. Thus we end up living a life of action without vision, in short, a life of dynamite — not dynamism.

A life of dynamism is one where all actions are performed without losing sight of the vision, which comes from quietude, contemplation, and inspiration. All the great masters spent a large part of their lives in solitude. What they did during that period is unknown to us, but history is replete with such examples. For instance, the life of Shankaracharya, was it not dynamic? His Guru, Govinda Bhagavadapada, who inspired him, spent all his life meditating on the banks of Narmada. Swami Vivekananda's life was very dynamic whereas his Guru, Swami Ramakrishna Paramahamsa, sat at one place — a Kali temple. Our Gurudev, Swami Chinmayananda's life was very dynamic but his Guru, Swami Tapovan spent a major part of his life in the Himalayas. Does this imply that the disciples were dynamic while the gurus were not? No, the Gurus' dynamism was far above normal activity. Swami Vivekananda was inspired on a rock at Kanyakumari and his achievements were tremendous. Bhagavan Ramana Maharshi stayed at one place, lived the life of a true hermit and inspired millions just by his mere presence. All this shows that real dynamism is different from what we usually perceive it to be.

A life of true dynamism is a life of vision, of inspiration and when these two are manifested in action, it becomes a source of inspiration for millions of people. This is not only true in the spiritual field, but in all other fields; like science, art, literature, and music. The lives of great masters in any field were full of contemplation and dynamism. That is precisely why they continue to inspire even after their death. The mere utterance of their names inspires so many people even today. Therefore it is said: The person, whose life becomes an inspiration to millions of people to lead a noble life, that person alone is said to be living. In contrast to this, we see others who live like birds to fill their bellies.

When we hear of a person's demise, we generally ask, "How did he die?" We never ask, "How did he live?" Our focus should be on what kind of life he lived. Did he live a life of inspiration or perspiration? When we look into the lives of great missionaries from different walks of life, we see that they have lived life in its true sense.

Therefore, what is this life of dynamism? This is most beautifully pointed out in the *Bhagavad Gītā*, particularly in the last verse. Sanjaya comments:

Only where Yogeshwara Lord Krishna and where bow-wielding Arjuna, (not the one who has discarded the bow) are together, there alone is wealth (*śrī*), victory (*vijaya*), and expansion (*bhūti*). (18:71)

A businessman always wants expansion, that is, greater development and prosperity. However, we will find prosperity only when we live according to the abiding values of life. There are two kinds of lives; one is the life of values and the other is a life of *valuables*. When we give too much importance to valuables then the values are put aside and when *values* are ignored, the person is devalued. When a person is rich, but without values then that person may have million dollars, but he'll still be a worthless person.

XIV

True Success
by Eckhart Tolle

Q: Is the notion of success just an egoic illusion? How do we measure true success?

A: The world will tell you that success is achieving what you set out to do. It will tell you that success is winning, that finding recognition and/or prosperity are essential ingredients in any success. All or some of the above are usually by-products of success, but they are not success. The conventional notion of success is concerned with the outcome of what you do. Some say that success is the result of a combination of hard work and luck, or determination and talent, or being in the right place at the right time. While any of these may be determinants of success, they are not its essence. What the world doesn't tell you because it doesn't know — is that you cannot *become* successful. You can only *be* successful. Don't let a mad world tell you that success is anything other than a successful present moment. And what is that? There is a sense of quality in what you do, even the most simple action. Quality implies care and attention, which come with awareness. Quality requires your Presence.

Let's say that you are a businessperson and after two years of intense stress and strain you finally manage to come out with a product or service that sells well and makes money. Success? In conventional terms, yes. In reality, you spent two years polluting your body as well as the earth with negative energy, made yourself and those around you miserable, and affected many others you never even met. The unconscious assumption behind all such action is that success is a future event, and that the end justifies the means. But the end and the means are one. And if the means did not contribute to human happiness, neither will the end. The outcome, which is inseparable from the actions that led to it, is already contaminated by those actions and so will create further unhappiness. This is karmic action, which is the unconscious perpetuation of unhappiness.

As you already know, your secondary or outer purpose lies within the dimension of time, while your main purpose is inseparable from the Now and therefore requires the negation of time. How are they reconciled? By realizing that your entire life journey ultimately consists of the step you are taking at this moment. There is always only this one step, and so you give it your fullest attention. This doesn't mean you don't know where you are going; it just means this step is primary, the destination secondary. And what you encounter at your destination once you get there depends on the quality of this one step. Another way of putting it: What the future holds for you depends on your state of consciousness now.

When doing becomes infused with the timeless quality of Being, *that* is success. Unless Being flows into doing, unless you are present, you lose yourself in whatever you do. You also lose yourself in thinking, as well as in your reactions to what happens externally.

XV

Right Attitudes for Success
by Swami Chinmayananda

You and I are alive; therefore we are active. As long as we are living, we have to act. Life pulsating through the body becomes activity in the outer world. Actions flow from living persons until death. It is important to understand how actions can be organized, altered and disciplined in order that they bring happiness to the community and a sense of fulfillment and satisfaction to the individual. This is called the "Art of Action."

Action is inevitable, because it is the signature of life. Life expresses itself in action as death does in inaction. But actions vary from person to person. A farmer working in the fields perspires and sweats with exertion. A poet in the midst of his greatest creation does not seem to be working at all from the farmer's point of view. From the standpoint of a poet, a scientist is wasting public money. From the scientist's standpoint, an ordinary thinker is wasting his time. From all their points of view Buddha sitting under a tree is an idler, an unnecessary leech upon society. Each one may point out to the other and say that he is an idler, but each one knows how vigorously he is working himself.

A great painter was once sitting near a wayside pool throwing stones into the water and watching the play of light and shade upon the ripples. An ordinary man, walking along the road, carrying milk to the nearby town jealously looked at the man and thought, "This fool is sitting idle from morning to evening, eating food that is brought to him. How unfair! I have already put in eight hours of work and I cannot make ends meet. What an injustice!"

The simple villager did not know that the person against whom he had complained was no less than Michelangelo, the great painter. As a result of observing the waves, he reproduced them on canvas. Michelangelo wanted to observe the play of light and shade on the waves so that he could capture their alluring beauty on canvas. He was vigorously studying, but others thought he was idling away his time. It was that man, the so called idler, who produced the immortal paintings and sculptures while the milkman worked and toiled honestly for society, died like a bug, leaving nothing for posterity to remember him by.

Everyone must work but what matters is how to work and in what way one should work. Being in the sun for the whole day alone is not work. That is only one method of work. The question is what type of work can we do and how can the maximum be brought out of us.

Working for Personal Gain

The great sages of ancient India observed that the type and quality of work people perform could be classified into three categories. The first of them is the lowest type and since I do not have a proper name, let us call it *laborer.* When I say laborer, I am not in any way bringing disgrace to the ordinary physical labor, I am not using the word in that sense.

The person who works in society only for the sake of wages and for profit is called a laborer. A great political leader of the country may be a laborer if he is putting forth his intelligence, body and mind for society with the idea that he will aggrandize more and more income for his personal gain. If you ask such a person why he wants wages, he has no motive greater than that he may furnish a beautiful home for his wife and children. The self-centered person works only for the profit that comes to him. He does not think of starting a hospital or serving society. He only wants to aggrandize more for his family. If that is the low ambition for which a person is pouring out his energy into the world, that person falls under the classification of a laborer.

In the same profession in which a laborer is working there can be another individual who is not a laborer. Next to Mahatma Gandhi who was inspired by the most selfless of ideals in the political field, we can see a laborer in the same political arena. It is not the field of work that matters. It is not the position that gives one dignity and glory to society; rather it is how one acts. If a person works with the idea that he will gain something from society that will benefit himself, this self-centered, limited point of view, even though he be a scientist, a great thinker, a writer or intellectually the greatest genius in the country, he is only a laborer from the philosophical point of view.

Working for an Ideal

In contrast to the laborer, the second variety is called a worker. What is the difference between a laborer and a worker? If one asks a worker why he is working he will say that he wants to bring about a change in society. His eyes are not on personal profit but on success for society. Success in what? Every worker has a picture of an ideal heaven or a perfect society. He will struggle hard in the world because he is inspired by a great enthusiasm and a great vision of life. He strives to bring that vision into actuality. He wants nothing else from life. He is ready to starve, he is ready to suffer but what he wants in the world is only success for his ideal. The political workers or the spiritual missionaries, the great cultural thinkers, all of them are struggling to bring the ideals they have into the world. To the extent the ideal is achieved, to that extent they are happy and feel that they have succeeded. Thus a laborer wants wages so that he and his wife and children may be comfortable. A worker, on the other hand, wants success for his ideal. He wants to bring it about in society.

Working with Joy

The third variety is very rare. Laborers are many in the world and the workers are less in number. But the third variety called the *Men of Achievement,* are very few indeed. It is these people who give a boost to the general cultural beauty of society and uplift the entire generation to a higher standard of life, a higher dignity of morality, and a greater virtue in living. Such mighty men are called saints and seers, prophets or incarnations of great virtues and values. They live an ideal life, inspiring others even after their death. The fragrance of their thought and the might and glory of their ideals gather a new momentum as the years pass by. Christ died two thousand years ago and yet we find that his glory becomes more and more compelling as time passes.

One may ask the man of achievement, "What is it that you want in the world, why are you working?" "Oh Buddha, why did you work? Oh Christ, why did you work? Oh Mohammed, why did you move from place to place preaching against many odds?" Men of achievement work in the world not for profit, nor for success, but from feeling that they are doing the right thing, irrespective of whether they are recognized or not in their lifetime. All that a man of achievement wants is the secret joy in himself. A sense of fulfillment that he did the best he could. He does not care whether others recognize him or not.

Men of fulfillment do not work for a more comfortable life nor do they work in the world to bring a heaven on earth but by practice and precept they try to lead mankind to live an ideal life. More often such men have been persecuted by society because they are too idealistic for their age. Against all obstacles, a man of fulfillment lives on inspiring others by his joyous way of life, and thus brings about a new movement of moral change in the country. In time the morality, the culture and civilization of the society rises up because of their work. Christ, Vivekananda, Shankara, they all gave impetus and force to the ideal — a life that they lived and experienced, not merely conceived and talked about.

Thus men of achievement are not mere laborers or workers but they are seekers of self-fulfillment. In spite of the fact that the people around them were not living, nor willing to live the ideal, they lived the idealistic life. They thrilled and inspired their generation, generating in them awe and a reverence for the perfect life. Such ideal individuals alone have uplifted the world to a higher level, to a greater consciousness of the higher joys in life.

PART THREE

The Leader

The wise leader is a resource for others,
He serves, supports, and nurtures
the people around him.

Tao Te Ching

If you can accept the role of a leader without the limelight, if you can trust the employees and quietly assure them that they have the resources to do their work, if you can be a resource yourself, then when your work is done, your employees will say — with wonder and enthusiasm that will carry over into the rest of their lives —"Amazing, We did it! All by ourselves!"

James A. Autry and Stephen Mitchell

Real Power: Business Lessons from the Tao Te Ching

Look at yourself as a spiritual being first, before you see yourself as a parent, husband, or as an executive. As an executive you cannot avoid stress that comes along with every project in your hand. But as a spiritual soul you are not responsible for any gain or loss in your life. Neither wealth nor health is perceived as permanent by a spiritual person. For him, handling stress is only handling a particular role efficiently, while he is always aware of the fact that he is not the role that he plays in the world.

Swami Ishwarananda

XVI

The Soul of Leadership
by Swami Nikhilananda

A leader is yourself embodied. He is the deepest core of your own being. He is the fulfillment of your desire. He is the joy of your heart, the inspiration behind your work, the dedication of your life. He is the spirit of the whole group. A leader is a seer. He can see in the future and make preparation to welcome it. He sees the dawn of morrow when the night is still dark. He is the silver lining of the dark clouds.

A leader is swift and agile like a deer. He dares to face challenges. He dares to dream the impossible. He dares to dream heaven on earth. He seals the bond among people. He is the link joining all. He empathizes with all and develops an instant rapport with people from different backgrounds. He is the smile of the distressed and the medicine of the sick. He is the song of those who have lost all hope. He is the game in children and optimism of the youth. He is the support for the old and solace for the sad.

A leader is at ease under all circumstances. Remaining at ease, he eases all. He dares to relax in the midst of chaos. He derives his strength from the inexhaustible source of inspiration within. He has direct communion with the leader of the entire world. A leader is a sincere, obedient follower of the Lord of all beings. A leader has tremendous faith in the higher values of life. He believes that God alone works through him.

A leader is very dear to all. He is seen as a friend, philosopher and guide. He sees the beauty in all and exposes the strength of others as a reed from a stalk. His area of influence is large, extending both in time and space. He is the real among the false. He is the changeless, among the changing. He is the common thread, among variety and differences.

A leader leads people through himself to the Supreme. He makes them live their dreams. He fulfils their innermost wish. He satisfies the very core of their being. He is a link between the present and the future. He is the link between the mundane and the fantastic. He is the bridge amongst the opposites. He is the bridge across the river of difficulties. He is the rising sun dispelling all darkness.

A leader is wise. He listens to the young and old. He listens to the silent cry in the heart of the lowly. He listens to the words of the divine among the mortals. A real leader is rare. He comes in an era and ere long transforms everything and everyone. In all leaders we find a spark from the eternal soul of leadership. Political leaders have it, the head of the family is guided by it. The scientist, the spiritual, the business leaders are all inspired by the same chord.

Everyone is a leader at his or her own level. There are people looking up to all of us. We derive our inspiration from some and we inspire others. Transformation in society, company, family and personal life has been brought about, when we are touched by such leaders. Leaders are inspired to transform their own lives and the lives of all those who come in contact with them.

May we discover such leadership within us and amongst others around us. May the soul of leadership flow through us to the world around us, transforming everyone on the way as the perennial Ganga which flows from the matted locks of Shiva; flowing on the plains of the country nourishing all on its way to the ocean!

XVII

Inspired Leadership
by Swami Chinmayananda

The leaders of humanity have a very subtle duty in life. They take upon themselves the difficult task of guiding the masses. To such dedicated men-of-action, Lord Krishna puts in a word of warning so that they may not cause any harm through excessive enthusiasm:

> Let no wise man unsettle the minds of the ignorant people who are attached to action; let him engage them in all actions, himself fulfilling them with devotion. (*Bhagavad Gītā,* 3:26)

A society is not built overnight through magic incantations. Time and tradition alone build up the strength and beauty of society. It is influenced both by the world-plan around and the personality-plan within. This scheme of things should not be suddenly altered. The art of guiding humanity without disrupting the existing harmony is well brought out by Lord Krishna in His note of warning to leaders in all fields. A true leader should fall in line with the generation, and slowly and steadily guide people to act in the right direction by setting an example for them to follow.

It is dangerous to unsettle the faith of the generation. Violent revolutions deform the character of the individual. History is replete with examples, where, in the excitement and enthusiasm following the discovery of new ideals, leaders have miscalculated the strength of the masses and have been destroyed by the very emotions and passions invoked by them earlier.

Krishna says that the best way to bring about a renaissance is by having the leaders of society express the Divinity in themselves, and thus attract a following. By precept and practice, the masses should be gradually guided toward the right path.

If one wants to be a good leader, one's first attempt should be to cultivate equanimity and poise within oneself, qualities that will raise one above the dualities in nature.

> The same in honor and dishonor, the same to friend and foe; abandoning all undertakings ... he is said to have crossed beyond the *guṇa*. (*Bhagavad Gītā*, 14:25)

Such a *karma yogin* crosses over and reaches beyond the shackles of the *guṇa: sattva, rajas*, and *tamas*. From such a noble person emanate the divine qualities of harmlessness, truth, renunciation, and fortitude. Having transcended the dualities, such a person is equally disposed towards friends and enemies; towards the indifferent neutrals and the hateful; towards relatives, both the righteous and the unrighteous.

When such noble leaders come forward to act in a spirit of co-operation and self-dedication, they release the community from its abject poverty, its harrowing sorrows, and from all the shackles of its ignorance, superstitions, and stupidities.

To arrive at such a balance within ourselves, and work in a spirit of dedication we have to free ourselves from attachment to the objects around us. Only in a mind freed from all its ego-centric burden, will calmness, poise, and equanimity take root. If universal love is to be cultivated, the sense of "I-ness" and "my-ness" should be burned away. Then comes the realization that his embodiment is only an instrument to carry out His will and must be carefully tuned to receive His grace. The following qualities belong to the one born to the Divine Estate, says Krishna:

> Fearlessness, purity of heart, steadfastness in the Yoga of Knowledge, alms-giving, control of the senses, sacrifice, study of the Scriptures, austerity, and straightforwardness, harmlessness, truth, absence of anger, renunciation, peacefulness,

absence of crookedness, compassion to beings, non-covetousness, gentleness, modesty, absence of fickle-mindedness, vigor, forgiveness, fortitude, purity, absence of hatred, absence of pride ... these belong to the one born for the Divine Estate, O Bharata. (*Bhagavad Gītā,* XVI:1-3)

A Glorious Example

As a leader, even after entering the vast field of work, one should not neglect one's obligatory duties. Such duties include those demanded of one's social status or domestic situation. As an example, Krishna points out to Arjuna the noble life of King Janaka, who set up a glorious example for his generation to follow. Because,

Whatever a great man does, other men imitate. Whatever he sets up as the standard that the world follows. (*Bhagavad Gītā,* 3:21)

Leaders should keep this in mind at all times and should engage in perfect actions that are well worth imitating. Illiterate masses who listen to the thundering eloquence of their leaders on platforms may not often understand the full import of their ideals, but they feel and appreciate the behavior and attitude of the leaders in society. These millions copy the decorum set as a standard by the leaders, not by their words but by their actions, and we know that these millions form the nation. Therefore, the rebuilding of a society or a country can be achieved only through the integrated character of its leaders. The true and vibrant personality capable of such achievements has been beautifully depicted by Krishna.

After due considerations, when one has put on the leader's mantle, one's first allegiance should be to the ideals one stands for. The ideals should be such that they inspire the masses to sink their mutual difference, work together, and strive with enthusiasm, bringing out mysterious qualities and quantities of dynamism in their individual endeavors to try to build unity and harmony. Amid the apparent diversity of work performed by each, there should not be any discordant notes.

Each action should be so perfect that it brings more and more peace and harmony into the environment. Only such actions can compose right service and come to reflect true dedication. One purges oneself of the accumulated burden of *vāsanā* through such actions. Through one's constant attunement with the higher and the nobler, one chastens one's personality. Such a polished personality is the right vehicle to work in this world of change and endless problems, for achieving success and happiness for generations to come.

XVIII

Moral Intelligence
by Doug Lennick and Fred Kiel

The time has come to openly acknowledge the contribution of moral intelligence to effective leadership and sustainability. Although both emotional intelligence and moral intelligence come into play when moral decisions are at stake, they are not the same. Emotional intelligence is values free. Moral intelligence is not. Emotional skills can be applied for good or evil. Moral skills, by definition, are directed toward doing good.

Emotional intelligence and moral intelligence, though distinct, are partners. Neither works in a truly effective way without the other. In *Primal Leadership: Realizing the Power of Emotional Intelligence,* Goleman and his co-authors, Richard Boyatzis and Annie McKee, tackle the boundary between emotional and moral intelligence when they discuss how good and bad leaders can use the same emotional competencies:

> Given that adept leaders move followers to their emotional rhythm, we face the disturbing fact that, throughout history, demagogues and dictators have used this same ability for deplorable ends. The Hitlers and Pol Pots of the world have all rallied angry mobs around a moving — but destructive-message. And therein lies the crucial difference between resonance and demagoguery...
>
> Demagoguery casts its spell via destructive emotions, a range that squelches hope and optimism as well as true innovation and creative imagination (as opposed to cruel cunning). By contrast, resonant leadership grounded in a shared set of constructive values keeps emotions resounding in the positive register. It invites people to take a leap of

faith through a word picture of what's possible, creating a collective aspiration[1].

Without a moral anchor, leaders can be charismatic and influential in a profoundly destructive way. As *Primal Leadership* emphasizes, truly effective leadership is "grounded in a shared set of constructive values."[2] Without knowledge of those values — in other words, moral intelligence — the skills of emotional intelligence are ultimately ineffective in promoting high performance.

Moral intelligence is not just important to effective leadership — it is the "central intelligence" for all humans. Why? It's because moral intelligence directs our other forms of intelligence to do something worthwhile. Moral intelligence gives our life purpose. Without moral intelligence, we would be able to do things and experience events, but they would lack meaning. Without moral intelligence, we wouldn't know why we do what we do — or even what difference our existence makes in the great cosmic scheme of things.

A Renewable Asset

The more you develop your moral intelligence, the more positive changes you will notice, not only in your work but in your personal well-being. Staying true to your moral compass will not eliminate life's inevitable conflicts. Will you have to compromise sometimes between your beliefs and the demands of your work environment? Yes! Will you make mistakes? Will you sometimes say the wrong thing out of jealousy or greed? Definitely! But staying the moral course will give you singular personal satisfaction and professional rewards.

Your "Moral Positioning System"

Think of moral intelligence as a "moral positioning system" for your life's journey, analogous to the global positioning system used in some cars as a navigational tool. You can be a great driver, and your car can have a powerful engine and four-wheel drive, but when it's dark and you've never been in this neck of the woods before, you have directions that were given you by someone who doesn't know street names, and you cannot see the map you got from AAA, you are lost. Despite all your tools and resources, you have no idea if you are headed in the right direction. But if your car had a global positioning system, it would be virtually impossible for you to get lost. Like having a GPS for your car, your moral intelligence allows you to better harness all your resources, your emotional intelligence, your technical intelligence, and your cognitive intelligence, to achieve the goals that are most important to you — whether on the job or in the rest of your life. Unlike today's GPSs, moral intelligence is not optional equipment. It is basic equipment for individuals who want to reach their best creative potential and business leaders who want to capture the best efforts of their workforce.

What Does Moral Intelligence Look Like?

Most successful leaders are morally gifted, but very few of them are moral geniuses. They all make mistakes from time to time and, earlier in their careers, they typically made moral mistakes more often. But because of their high moral intelligence, they were quick studies. They held themselves accountable for their moral lapses, learned from them, and moved on. Consider Jay Coughlan's story. Today, Coughlan is the CEO of Lawson Software, but no one would have predicted his rise to that top spot back in 1998 after he fell asleep while driving intoxicated, causing a devastating accident that left him seriously injured and his father dead. The accident was the beginning of a remarkable personal transformation marked by a reawakening of his religious faith, a stronger relationship with his family and involvement in the community, and an intensive commitment to Lawson. Coughlan pleaded guilty to vehicular homicide and was sentenced to one month in jail, five months of house arrest, and 10 years of probation. But because of Coughlan's honesty and the support of the community, the judge reduced his offense to a misdemeanor after he had served over three months of his sentence. Meanwhile, during his absence from Lawson, the health care division that Coughlan had launched was flourishing. "That's when I learned I actually was successful as a leader," he told *The Wall Street Journal*, "when you can pull yourself out of the machine and it can still run."[3] His financial results were impressive and likely were the most significant factor in his subsequent promotions. The accident would have been a career-ending event for most people in Coughlan's shoes, but his response to the accident was extraordinary. "Jay, to his credit, stood right up and took responsibility; there was no hesitation," says Richard Lawson, the company's chairman and former CEO. "To me that is what counts. It's not the mistakes you make, it's how you react to those mistakes."

Lynn Fantom, CEO of ID Media, the largest direct response media service company in the U.S., is another morally gifted leader. It is late in the afternoon one cool spring day when Lynn walks back to her corner office in a New York City skyscraper. The Empire State Building is visible out one window, the Met Life and Flat Iron building out the other. Lynn barely notices the spectacular view. She goes straight to her desk and opens an e-mail from a Human Resources manager at her parent company, Interpublic. HR, it seems, is worried about how overloaded she is. They wonder if it is the best use of her time to respond to the employee comments and questions she gets on the "Ask Lynn" column on the company's intranet. Her public relations folks are also concerned about her schedule. They've recommended that she stop spending precious time posting her thoughts on media and marketing trends on the intranet. But Lynn thinks her personal responses to employees are an important part of the ID Media culture. She thinks that "Ask Lynn" gives her an opportunity to demonstrate that she cares about her workforce. She thinks that she has a responsibility to her workforce to share her business insights. To her, it's time well spent. Lynn is certain that employees like knowing they can ask her about anything and that she will give them an honest response. They also like knowing that she understands market trends and shares her understanding with them. "In exchange," says Lynn, "I really get their commitment to help us succeed." Lynn is sticking to her principles. She won't be giving up her intranet contributions anytime soon.

Moral Intelligence and Business Success

Though leaders may attribute their companies' success to their commitment to moral principles, their evidence is based only on their personal experiences. So far, there has been no quantitative research that specifically studied the business impact of moral intelligence. But there are objective indications that moral intelligence is critical to the financial performance of your business. One measure of the influence of moral intelligence on business results comes from American Express Financial Advisors, an American Express company that implemented a highly effective emotional competence training program. American Express defined *emotional competence* as "the capacity to create alignment between goals, actions, and values." The program emphasized development of self-leadership and interpersonal effectiveness and demonstrated how those emotional skills led to business and personal success. The bottom line impact of the program was impressive, with participants in a pilot group producing sales that were 18 percent higher than a control group that didn't have the benefit of the training — no small change in a company that managed or owned assets in excess of $232 billion at the time. At the heart of the program was a special subset of skills that helped people to discover their principles and values and then create goals and action steps that flowed from those deeply held principles and values. American Express Financial Advisors' leaders came to realize that it was this overriding moral framework, that is, the emphasis on *principles* and *values*, that accounted for much of the success of the program. American Express had already found from internal studies that the most successful advisors were highly confident, resilient under adverse circumstances, and, most importantly, acted from a strong core of principles and values. To form trusting partnerships with clients, advisors needed to be genuinely trustworthy. To be seen as trustworthy, advisors had to act in accordance with worthwhile personal values. If advisors practiced the self-management and social skills they learned in the training, but failed to operate from moral principles and values, they would fall short of sustainable success.

While American Express' data demonstrates the importance of an individual advisor's moral intelligence to financial performance, other businesses have discovered that they produce the best results when their company overall is known for its moral intelligence. Market research tells us that consumers judge a company's reputation mainly on the basis of its perceived values. A company's reputation translates straight to the bottom line: Consumers prefer to make purchases from companies who are known for their ethical practices."[4]

The business case for moral intelligence gets another boost from a study done at DePaul University in Chicago. Researchers from the School of Accountancy and MIS compared the financial performance of 100 companies selected by *Business Ethics* magazine as "Best Corporate Citizens" with the performance of the rest of the S&P 500. Corporate citizenship rankings were based on quantitative measures of corporate service to seven stakeholder groups: stockholders, employees, customers, the community, the environment, overseas stakeholders, and women and minorities. The study found that overall financial performance of the 2001 Best Corporate Citizen companies was significantly better than the rest of the S&P 500. The average performance of the Best Citizens, as measured by the 2001 *Business Week* rankings of total financial performance, was more than 10 percentile points higher than the mean rankings of the rest of the S&P 500. According to *Strategic Finance* magazine, which reported the study, "It casts doubt on the persistent myth that good citizenship tends to lead to additional costs and thus negatively impacts a firm's financial results."[5]

FOOTNOTES:

[1]   Daniel Goleman, Richard Boyatzis, Annie McKee, *Primal Leadership: Realizing the Power of Emotional Intelligence,* Harvard Business School Press, 2002.

[2]   Ibid.

[3]   Reported in Marcelo Prince, "Manager Discovers Leadership in an Accident's Aftermath," *The Wall Street Journal,* April 5, 2002.

[4]   Cone/Roper Cause Related Trends Report, 1999.

[5]   *Strategic Finance,* Vol. 83, No. 7, p. 20, January 2002.

XIX

The Role of a Leader
by Azim Premji

The only sustainable advantage of any business is its talent, because everything else can be very easily and quickly replicated in today's competitive world. The theme of the conference is thus very appropriate and relevant. The topic I have been asked to speak on Values and Leadership — is even closer to my heart. It has been my own experience that there cannot be any leadership without values.

Fortunately, there is no longer any debate about it. When we at Wipro defined our beliefs in the early Seventies, many people would ask me whether values come in the way of success. We insisted that values not only help in achieving success but also make success more enduring and lasting. They help establish business or career purposes. Values combined with a powerful vision can turbo-charge us to scale new heights and make us succeed beyond our wildest expectations.

Recent events bear testimony to this. Financial and business scandals have had very serious and long-term consequences; leave aside the financial loss. If you look only at the collateral damage due to loss of confidence in the economy, the cost of each scandal reaches astronomical proportions. Paul Krugman, a leading economist and one of the prominent contenders for the Nobel Prize, feels that the damage done by these scandals to the US economy is far greater in American history than the cataclysmic events of September 11, 2001. Similarly, those who abide by values have always seemed to gain. Studies of firms in India and abroad have shown that markets and investors take notice of well-managed companies, respond positively to them, and reward such companies with higher valuations.

The simple truth is that all business revolves around trust. We need to have the trust of our customers, shareholders and certainly the talent that works with us. Unfortunately, trust is fragile in nature. It takes years of effort to build trust but only a few acts to destroy it. Once it is broken, it is even harder to rebuild.

No regulatory or legal body can ever ensure trust and no act by itself can guarantee ethical behavior. It can only be addressed through effective leadership code that permeates the organization. Leaders must understand that their primary job is not so much to create profits as to create a culture of values. With embedded values, business becomes easier and less prone to sudden collapse.

The first benefit is that values help to attract the right kind of people you want to do business with. I think there are honest people everywhere. When they do business with you, they feel energized. Nothing strengthens business relationships as shared values. At the same time, it repels those whose values may be different. They keep away from you. And if they cannot keep away, they do business with you on your terms! They may try once or twice to influence you to their way of doing business, but once they find you unyielding and firm, they stop doing that because the effort is futile. After that, one can continue doing business unhampered.

Second, values can serve as a strong anchor and help us weather the uncertainties in business. Business has been going through turbulent times even without the scams. It began with the changing landscape of the market and competitive landscape due to globalization. Then came the economic downturn and recession, which led to many companies closing shop after decades of success. Values help us not to get washed away by passing waves, because they help us to keep our feet on firm ground.

Thirdly, values provide us with focus and courage to stand

up to any distractions along the way. The strong desire to move ahead can at times tempt businesses to cut corners or bend rules. Values provide the necessary brakes or limits to keep leadership from going astray. Values essentially provide us with an internal discipline.

Finally, values form the essence of all relationships. Values can be a powerful cementing force between people who think alike. Ultimately this builds a great team and even if there are differences between people, they are submerged in the larger group interests. It also provides them with super-ordinate goals that motivate them beyond reward and recognition.

What do I mean by values? Let me share with you values that we have defined for Wipro and also some personal values that have a lot of meaning for me. They are by no means comprehensive, but I hope they will be of use to you.

The Four Values

At Wipro, we have articulated four values. All of them are equally important and not ranked in the order I am mentioning them.

First is — *human values*. This means that we respect customers and employees as individuals, recognize that they have different needs and continually strive towards satisfying those needs to improve the quality of their lives.

The second is — *integrity*. We believe strongly that all our individual and business relationships will be governed by the highest standards of integrity.

Third is constantly providing — *innovative solutions*. We believe in constantly researching and developing superior products and services that meet the ever-changing needs of the customers.

The fourth is — *value for money*. We believe that we must constantly deliver value for whatever the customer pays us. The customer must always feel that he or she experiences continuous improvement in quality, cost and delivery of our products and services rendered. These values are so important that they define every decision and action we take.

Personal Values

In addition to these, I always believed in a few personal values that make leaders different from others. Let me share some of these with you.

First is the value of *hard work*. We have to become a nation of hard workers. It was not resources but hard work that transformed other nations such as Japan and China. Steady work builds up both wealth and power and keeps one's conscience in rectitude. We need to work hard and work smart. We have to change from our image of India, from being a nation of holidays to a nation of people who enjoy hard work.

Second is the value of *self-confidence*. Centuries of subjugation has made us embrace a fatalistic approach to life. But that is all in the past. The millennium of the mind has altered the entire landscape of competitive advantage. India has one of the largest pools of disciplined, technical talent. It has won enormous respect from nations all over the world, whether it is in information technology, scientific research or in academia. Self-confidence has to be an intrinsic part of our approach in demanding what is due for our merit and ability. We should not undersell ourselves to the outside world, no matter what our internal competitive compulsions may be. The truth is that nobody can make us feel inferior without our consent.

The third value is *humility*. Humility is not opposed to self-confidence. In fact, though it might seem like a paradox, people with the highest self-confidence have the highest humility because they have nothing to prove to themselves. Humility is a pre-requisite for continuous learning from any environment. No matter how good you are, someone out there knows how to do things a little better. Technology keeps changing and standards of excellence keep getting upgraded. If we have humility, we develop an open mind to absorb the changes. Remember, the mind is like a parachute. It functions only when it is open.

The fourth value is *persistence*. There are enough stories of people who gave up their search for gold and stopped digging just a few feet away from the gold ore deposit. Nothing is ever achieved in one go. One has to keep at it irrespective of the initial setbacks and frustration. You owe it to yourself to make that one more try that could make all the difference.

Finally, we must remember that values are what we practice and demonstrate and not what we speak about. Values must become part of an "internal voice" and not what we listen to when someone is watching. Mahatma Gandhi said a long time ago, "Do not install a light on your bicycle because the policeman is looking. Do it because you want to see well."

There is a story about the famous musician Tansen, who lived in the court of Emperor Akbar. One day, the Emperor asked Tansen whether he had a teacher who had developed this art in him. Tansen replied that he had a teacher called Swami Haridas. The Emperor said, "If you can sing so well, I am sure your teacher can sing even better. Please call him." Tansen replied that his teacher would never agree to come to the Emperor' s court. If he wanted to hear the teacher, they would have to go to him. Both Emperor Akbar, disguised as Tansen's friend, and Tansen went to the forest where the teacher lived. Swami Haridas greeted them warmly and requested them to stay with him. Tansen said that his friend had come with him to hear the teacher. Swami Haridas smiled. For the next few days nothing happened and Emperor Akbar began to get restless. Suddenly, one night, the teacher started singing. The Emperor was stunned because he had never heard anything like that before. He listened spellbound. Unfortunately, when he went to meet the teacher in the morning to tell him about how wonderful the song was, Swami Haridas was nowhere to be found. Tansen was sad. He told the Emperor that since he had brought a stranger there, his teacher had left the house for good. Tansen and the Emperor returned. The Emperor continued to be pensive. Finally, he asked Tansen whether the teacher had taught him what he sang. Tansen said he had and sang the same tune. At the end of it, the Emperor said, "You are one of the greatest singers I know. Yet between you and your teacher there is a gap. The magic I heard when he sang is not there in what you sing." Tansen smiled and said, "It is true. I sing for thee. But he sings for himself and the Divine Being within him."

True leadership is not just about inculcating values. It is about allowing people to experience the magic of what they stand for. Then nobody has to tell others what to do and, certainly, nobody has to watch over them.

XX

Right Intention
by Nancy Spears

"Correct all wrongs with one intention" - Atisha Dipankara Shrijnana

By instilling the *Buddha:* 9 *to* 5 approach to management, you make a choice to take the high road and elevate your corporate consciousness with deliberate intention. You decide to examine and fine-tune corporate and personal missions. In essence, you commit to set the Right Intention and to wake up your organization.

When you and your employees carry a sense of commitment that is driven by an intention to make a positive impact, you cultivate a personal power that goes beyond the job itself. You set a tone of confidence and dedication that stems from the root of your mission, the Right Intention. It is this intention that drives the day-to-day effort and ignites excitement in the workplace.

Once ignited, your company's mission will serve as a beacon that illuminates the way to making healthy decisions. You and your employees can focus on the work itself with a newly kindled inspiration. By tuning in and establishing an awareness of your intention, you will seed a path that flourishes with inspiration and prosperity.

Having the courage to walk this path requires working with your inherent intelligence and genuine basic goodness. Our wisdom, our intelligence, is what we often refer to as the "little voice" that we hear in the back of our mind. Although we frequently opt to ignore it, the voice is always present and can be accessed at any time. It is pure, luminous and unbiased. It tells us what is real. It is our wisdom. This wisdom is the consciousness of the Buddha nature that resides in all of us. When we access this nature, we are said to be waking up!

Mindful Awareness Exercise

Begin to set the Right Intention with a few tough but honest questions. Ask yourself:

- Does my company offer a motivating, creative, open environment for employees to do good work with passion?
- Are our employees committed to making a difference by contributing uniquely to the success of our company?
- Does this organization function as if it is awake?

The Four Immeasurables of a Leader

The foundation of your mission statement should represent your core qualities. Buddhism provides us with a practice that calls up these qualities, and provides a template for the core of your mission termed the Four Immeasurables, the practice generates a genuine ability to soften and broaden your view about your place in the world, and therefore access your Buddha nature. These four qualities serve as your non-negotiables and are the core of your mission. The Four Immeasurables in the context of Buddha in the workplace and boardroom are:

Loving Kindness. When we relate to our self or another person from a place of loving kindness, we ask for happiness to surround them and us. The loving-kindness practice affirms: "May all beings enjoy happiness and the root of happiness."

When we consciously declare thoughts of loving kindness, we connect with our authentic self to cultivate that success and happiness. In the business model, this quality requires that we work with a positive intention to serve ourselves and others in the organization ethically, generously, and with kindness. In situations that involve negotiations, loving-kindness takes off the edge of aggression and clears the way for open communications.

Compassion. Compassion is the conduit to increasing the growth of your organization and for impacting the world. The basis of compassion is to stay open enough to feel the pain or needs of others, which expands your view beyond your personalized, absorbed self.

When you access your compassion, you communicate from the heart, and that communication transcends the borders of hierarchy and position to allow for the flow of effortless creativity. As you write your mission statement with a mindset of compassion, you can see how your efforts in human resources, sales, research and development, customer service, and so on contribute to the health of your organization and the world at large.

When a mission statement demonstrates compassion, a natural cycle of prosperity is created. The CEO and board direct the organization with values and genuine caring, which in turn motivates the employees and enhances productivity and which ultimately increases profitability and growth. This cycle of management by compassion then flows full circle back to the shareholders, CEO, and board.

Joy. When you practice a joyful mindset, you delight in the happiness and success of others and eliminate the need or temptation for jealousy and aggression. Joy promotes a vibrant work culture internally and externally. When you and your organization practice joy, you ask that, "All beings not be separated from their own happiness, free from suffering."

In this sense, the mission and values of the organization acknowledge a goal to enjoy prosperity and success and to use the benefits of that success responsibly and with integrity. Thus, this practice guards against the risk of the inappropriate use of profits, pension plans, and other improprieties that would negatively affect the employees, management, and shareholders of a corporation.

Equanimity. Equanimity allows us to accept the good and the bad in all situations; having the peace of mind that everything is workable. When managers engage the quality of equanimity, they establish a motivated work environment that engages everyone in their department or company. Equanimity also provides a workplace free of prejudice or discrimination, and this freedom encourages open-minded thinking and cultivates innovation.

In this practice we ask that, "All beings dwell in equanimity free from passion, aggression, and prejudice." Equanimity is an essential condition of a values-driven mission. It expands the possibility for growth and opens the doorway to attracting new talent and knowledge that will be recycled into the organization.

XXI

Inclusiveness

by Susan Smith Kuczmarski
and Thomas D. Kuczmarski

Dipak Jain serves on the board of directors of John Deere and Company, yet he does not know how to drive a car let alone a tractor. He has consulted for IBM, Motorola, and U.S. Cellular, yet prefers old-fashioned technology. He is charged with molding the next generation of business leaders, a traditionally blood-thirsty lot, yet he is a vegetarian who preaches nonviolence.

Introspective and humble, Dipak Jain seems an unlikely choice to guide those aspiring to reach the upper echelons of the corporate world. Yet, since taking over as dean of Northwestern University's Kellogg School of Management in July 2001, Jain has utilized his global perspective and commitment to innovation to build the program's reputation as the world's premier business school. Kellogg was voted the "Best Business School" a record five consecutive times in Business Week's *survey of U.S. business schools. Jain views inclusiveness as a core value — one that can be seen when he often greets others with a hug. He demonstrates that even in the cutthroat world of business, valuing the diverse perspectives and contributions of all people is what effective and values-based leadership is all about....*

Lifting People Up

Not only do effective leaders grasp the value of inclusiveness, they take it to the ultimate — they lift people up.

"I strongly believe that when you work with people you need to know how to lift them up," says Jain. "You need to create an environment where people feel that you really inspire and lift them to a higher level. In turn, they should feel good working with you because they know they will be valued. They will also have an opportunity to move up — professionally, personally, and emotionally. The whole concept of an environment that lifts people up is very important. It lets those around you see that working together helps everyone rise together, and that is where you develop a sense of inclusiveness with your people."

Jain believes that the key is to view others in a business as working *with* you and not *for* you. When leaders consider themselves separate from other employees, they create inherent conflict within the organization. They limit their resources, and in so doing, limit the amount that the team as a whole is able to achieve.

Jain also believes that humility works hand-in-hand with inclusiveness. Recall his analogy: "As fruit ripens, its tree starts bending down. This means that as you move up in life, you need to become more humble and more down to earth. You need to point more toward the earth than toward the sky."

Inclusiveness is a leadership characteristic that is often hard to come by. Diversity programs within companies and organizations are only one step. Securing a mix of different types of people is a good start, but true progress is when managers make a diverse mix of people feel included, valued, and important to the overall goals and mission of the organization. Dipak Jain acts as if inclusiveness was a natural and normal thing to do. It should be.

Why Be Inclusive?

Though families in India are very inclusive, Indian society is segregated. Much of the country still operates under a caste system that separates individuals into different professional and socioeconomic classes. To a large extent, this hierarchy encourages those at the top to look down upon those below.

While Dipak Jain is Indian, he holds the belief that all souls are equal. His last name is derived from Jainism, the religion that he practices, a subset of Hinduism that preaches nonviolence. While his native country still operates under ancient tenets that promote division, Jain advocates a more participatory, transparent, and inclusive organizational structure.

"I come from a culture that is purely hierarchical," Jain says. "And coming from that culture, I feel that hierarchy is wrong because I have seen that style of management lead to more rather than fewer problems. And one thing I learned is that if you are in a hierarchal system, what is important is the people that work with you. They also need to be taken into consideration — they need to have a voice. They have to be a part of the overall decision-making process. Now, you can never reach total consensus, you can never please everyone. If you are soliciting information and you don't do anything with it, you can create more unhappiness. The best organizations create a culture where there is transparency and openness in the system. You promote a sense of fairness and integrity. I have my own personal saying: 'the outcome or the result is the sight, the process of reaching the outcome is the insight.'"

Hierarchies isolate us from each other. They stifle the exchange of ideas and the collective power of teams. The limiting aspect of this rigid structure is not lost on workers. When employees know that there is no system in place for their voices to be heard, what confidence will they have that a leader has all the information necessary to make the best decision?

"The moment you take a hierarchical approach, you have created a problem," Jain explains. "People are not sure whether you are saying what you believe, or saying what you are supposed to because of your position. So, people get confused. Is the message you are sending the real message or the one you think should be delivered?

"If you explain the decision-making process that you went through, then when people see the result, they will buy into it because they know this is how it happened. The process has to be transparent to the system. That is how we need to do things.

You don't have to say, I talked to Mr. Smith and not to Mr. Jones; that's not the point. There is a way for people to contribute, to say: 'my ideas and thoughts all went into the decision, my inputs got included, and the output was something that I was a part of.'"

Sadly, exclusion reigns in many workplaces. However, when inclusiveness exists within an organization, individuals feel attached and connected. They know that they belong and play an important role in the growth of their organization. They are involved in shaping the culture in which they work.

How is an Inclusive Culture Created?

Many times, culture entails one thing to senior management and something very different to employees. Inclusiveness means to give people a voice. At work, employees should feel that a decision was not a one-person pronouncement. There must be opportunities for group members to listen to others and contribute. Most people need to know that their comments are heard and their contributions are valued. When making a decision, leaders should be able to say: "I listened to everyone; this is what I heard; this is what I am doing; and this is why I am doing it." This creates a culture of inclusiveness.

There are four components for creating inclusive organizational cultures: play the game to "win-win," remember where you came from, harness the human potential, and eliminate complications.

Play the Game to "Win-Win"

Most leaders view business as a zero-sum game. For every winner, there must be a loser. Society celebrates those who are able to secure advantageous deals, even at the expense of others. In boardrooms around the world, you will hear a lot of talk of profits, earnings, and growth. Sadly, thinks Jain, you rarely hear discussion of mutual respect and love.

"My personal values structure is that when I deal with people or organizations, it has to be a win-win scenario," he reveals. "At the end, what you want to be left with is a sense that you are right for each other. After you hire someone, the person should feel very strongly about your organization, and you should feel very strongly about him or her. This is important. I am a big believer in a values system that prevents you from thinking that you got more than the other person. That to me is the start of a problem and not a solution."

Jain recognizes that business deals are not simply about the numbers on the balance sheets. There are people involved and relationships at stake. Decisions are not made in a vacuum, and leaders must be aware of the consequences of their actions.

Remember Where You Came From

Jain was raised in northeast India in the village of Tezpur, where as a child he sat quietly on the floor of his school soaking in the daily lessons. As a graduate student and professor at the remote Gauhati University, he wrote to scholars in the United States to obtain copies of journals and research papers. It was his curiosity and willingness to look beyond his surroundings that eventually brought him to the University of Texas at Dallas to pursue his PhD.

He has lived in America for more than two decades, but Jain returns to southeast Asia often. He values the sense of community and respect for others that exists in Asian cultures.

"We are blessed in one dimension that in the Indian system, we all live together," he says. "We have a joint family system. And I tell you a joint family system is basically an organization. We have four brothers, and they all live together. The father is there, he is the head of the family. We four brothers are like four consultants. There is no hierarchy there. We have our families, we have our children. Each one has to serve its own interest, but we all live together so it becomes like a miniature organization."

The school Jain now heads is a far cry from the crowded, impoverished classroom of his youth. Yet despite his success,

Jain always remembers the journey it took for him to arrive at his current position.

"People tend to forget history," he says. "History is an incredibly important thing. You need to know how you arrived here today. How did you reach this outcome? History is where all the insights are. You need to take time and consider what you have done to reach this position. Most of the values we hold, they come from how we were brought up. They come from our parents and our community and we must never forget the influence that they have had on us."

This dichotomy, the need to study the past in order to ensure a better future, is at the heart of effective leadership. It is this willingness to learn, this desire to push forward and tackle new challenges that has served Jain so well.

Dipak Jain still feels very much a part of his family, country, village, school, and faculty. In the same way that he feels very much a part of each these groups, he too tries to make each of them part of him. Inclusiveness is an indispensable watchword for truly effective leaders.

Harness the Human Potential

For a man who operates in a world of acquisitions and accumulation, Jain talks a lot about looking at what we already have.

"I think in business schools we need to have courses that let individuals focus on their inner strengths," Jain suggests. "We have not done a good job harnessing the potential that lies within a human being. And we need to do a good job, because everyone in the world is talented, they have lots to offer but nobody takes the time to dig within themselves. What we all tend to search for and seek out are outward values as opposed to seeing what is already within yourselves."

Jain sees this outward focus as largely self-destructive. Too much energy is spent on jealously, greed, and desire. In looking at others before we look at ourselves, we forsake the gifts that ought to be the easiest and most gratifying to cultivate.

Eliminate Complications

Often leaders try to be all things to all people. There is a perception that they must be experts on everything related to an organization. However, the result is often an individual who knows very little about a lot of things. Jain believes leaders should determine who they serve and focus on delivering for those audiences. This prevents confusion and increases confidence from co-workers.

"I believe strongly that one should lead as simple a life as possible because all the complications that you bring in effect your performance. So, when you say your purpose in life is to do things well, you have moral duties to the different segments of your life you serve. In my case, it's the students, it's my staff, it's my family, and it's my faculty. I need to make sure they feel respected, loved, benefit from my leadership and that I do my best for them. I cannot satisfy everyone, that also I know for sure. However, people should know where I stand and why I do things the way I do."

Jain is not a person that believes in optimization. He says: "I don't go through life saying I want to achieve this, I want to be here, or I want to be there. I have a very simple rule: whatever is given to me, I do it in the best possible manner. Let others be the judge if they want to put me in a particular place. Because once you keep doing things with your whole conscience and with your full effort rewards will be there. So, my mission in life is very simple. I am not a person who believes in too much materialism."

PART FOUR

The Workplace

*Common values, based in the universal principles,
can knit together a diverse global workforce.*

Doug Lennick and Fred Kiel

A sense of harmony and cohesiveness in an organization can arise only when the members are truly inspired with the goal of the institution and work in a dedicated manner to achieve it. Such organizations alone can stand firm against all external pressures, because within there is a team of hardy members holding together and functioning as many hands but with one head and heart. The members and office bearers, as executives, work in an organization in a common spirit of joyous excitement, from which unity of purpose, tireless enthusiasm, cheerful pursuit and such other virtues arise.

This is called *Karma Yoga* as described in the *Bhaga-vad Gītā*, functioning in the *Yajña* spirit. It is the ego and its selfish desires in our hearts that compel us to break the homogenous harmony and the joyful rhythm in the day-to-day working of an institution. Unless the dedication of the members to the idea for which the institution strives is firm and faithful, the best in them cannot stream forth to enrich the total achievement of the institution.

Swami Chinmayananda

XXII

The Seven Pillars
of an Organization
by Radhakrishnan Pillai

Kautilya's *Arthaśāstra* is the oldest book on Management available to the world. It was written by Kautilya (also known as Chanakya and Vishnugupta) in 300 B.C. Literally translated it means "Scripture of Wealth." The main focus of the book is on creation and management of wealth. However, the book is a masterpiece which covers a wide range of topics like statecraft, politics, military warfare, strategy, selection and training of employees, leadership skills, legal systems, accounting systems, taxation, fiscal policies, civil rules, internal and foreign trade and so on. It also covers various technical subjects including medicine, gemology, metallurgy, measures of length, tables of weights, divisions of time, among many others.

No wonder scholars down the centuries have time and again described Kautilya as a rare mastermind who could be an expert in so many varied and specialized fields.

He was responsible to bring down the Nanda dynasty and establish his able student Chandragupta Maurya on the throne as the emperor. Hence he is called a King Maker. He is also credited to have masterminded the defeat of Alexander in India when he was on his march to conquer the world.

As a political thinker, he was the first to visualize the concept of a *nation* for the first time in human history. During his time India was split into various kingdoms. He brought all of them together under one central governance, thus creating a nation called *āryāvarta,* which later became India. He documented his life-long work in this book *Arthaśāstra.* For ages rulers across the world have referred to the *Arthaśāstra* for building a nation on sound economics, based on spiritual values. Emperor Ashoka is supposed to have built and expanded his kingdom on the principles described in this book. Shivaji, the ruler of Maharashtra is said to have studied this book in order to plan and defeat the Mughals. The Forts that he built and the navy he created till today stands as an example for all of us to be proud of.

Even though India and Indians never forgot the *Arthaśāstra,* the study and practical application of the book lost its importance since the British rule.

Prof. Shama Shastry rediscovered the book in 1905, and wrote its first English translation. Ever since then, only two more English translations have been written. One by Prof. Kangle and the other by Shri Rangarajan.

However, apart from the scholarly work this book today needs to be once again represented for practical application in today's world. The book has got many principles and techniques, which once applied can prove a tremendous improvement even in our day-to-day management.

Some may ask "Is this book written over 2000 years ago still applicable in today's world?" For which great thinkers have said, "The *Arthaśāstra* is a book about the management of the human mind, which has remained the same in all ages. As long as the human mind remains filled with its negativities of jealousy, ego, hatred and over-indulgence. As long as human beings require self-control, discipline and management, Kautilya's *Arthaśāstra* will remain relevant."

Looking at the Seven Pillars

In the following verse Kautilya lists seven pillars for an organization:

The king, the minister, the country, the fortified city, the treasury, the army and the ally are the constituent elements of the state. (6:1.1)

Let us now take a closer look at each of them:

1. The King (The leader)

All great organizations have great leaders. The leader is the visionary, the captain, the man who guides the organization. In today's corporate world we call him the Director or the CEO. Without him we will loose direction.

2. The Minister (The manager)

The manager is the person who runs the show — the second-in-command of an organization. He is also the person whom you can depend upon in the absence of the leader. He is the man who is always in action. An extra-ordinary leader and an efficient manager together bring into existence a remarkable organization.

3. The Country (Your market)

No business can exist without its market capitalization. It is the area of your operation. The place from where you get your revenue and cash flow. You basically dominate this territory and would like to keep your monopoly in this segment.

4. The Fortified City (Head office)

You need a control tower — a place from where all planning and strategies are made. It's from here that your central administrative work is done. It's the nucleus and the center of any oranization.

5. The Treasury

Finance is an extremely important resource. It is the backbone of any business. A strong and well-managed treasury is the heart of any organization. Your treasury is also your financial hub.

6. The Army (Your team)

When we go to war, we need a well-equipped and trained army. The army consists of your team members. Those who are ready to fight for the organization. The salesmen, the accountant, the driver, the peon — all of them add to your team.

7. The Ally (friend / consultant)

In life you should have a friend who is just like you. Being, in the same boat, he can identify with you and stay close. He is the one whom you can depend upon when problems arise. After all, a friend in need is a friend in deed.

Look at these seven pillars. Only when these are built into firm and strong sections can the organization shoulder any responsibility and face all challenges. And while building them do not forget to imbibe that vital ingredient called values.

XXIII

Core Values of
Visionary Companies

by Jim Collins and Jerry I. Porras

Core values are the organization's essential and enduring tenets, not to be compromised for financial gain or short-term expediency. Thomas J. Watson, Jr., former IBM chief executive, commented on the role of core values (what he calls beliefs) in his 1963 booklet *A Business and Its Beliefs*:

> I believe the real difference between success and failure in a corporation can very often be traced to the question of how well the organization brings out the great energies and talents of its people. What does it do to help these people find common cause with each other? ... And how can it sustain this common cause and sense of direction through the many changes which take place from one generation to another? ... [I think the answer lies] in the power of what we call *belief* and the appeal these beliefs have for its people .... I firmly believe that any organization, in order to survive and achieve success, must have a sound set of beliefs on which it premises all its policies and actions. Next, I believe that the most important single factor in corporate success is faithful adherence to those beliefs ... *Beliefs must always come before policies, practices, and goals. The latter must always be altered if they are seen to violate fundamental beliefs.*[1]

In most cases, a core value can be boiled down to a piercing simplicity that provides substantial guidance. Notice how Sam Walton captured the essence of Wal-Mart's number one value:

"[We put] the customer ahead of everything else …. If you're not serving the customer, or supporting the folks who do, then we don't need you."[2] Notice how James Gamble simply and elegantly stated P&G's core value of product quality and honest business: "When you cannot make pure goods of full weight, go to something else that is honest, even if it is breaking stone."[3] Notice how John Young, former HP chief executive, captured the simplicity of the HP Way: "The HP Way basically means respect and concern for the individual; it says 'Do unto others as you would have them do unto you.' That's really what it's all about."[4] The core value can be stated a number of different ways, yet it remains simple, clear, straightforward, and powerful.

Visionary companies tend to have only a few core values, usually between three and six. In fact, we found none of the visionary companies to have more than six core values, and most have less. And, indeed, we should expect this, for only a few values can be truly *core* — values so fundamental and deeply held that they will change or be compromised seldom, if ever.

This has important implications for articulating core values in your own organization. If you list more than five or six values, you might not be capturing those that are truly core. If you have a statement of corporate values, or are in the process of creating one, you might ask yourself: "Which of these values would we strive to live to for a hundred years *regardless* of changes in the external environment — *even* if the environment ceased to reward us for having these values, or perhaps even penalized us? Conversely, which values would we be willing to change or discard if the environment no longer favored them?" These questions can help you identify which values are authentically core.

A very important point: We strongly encourage you *not* to fall into the trap of using the core values from the visionary companies as a source for core values in your own organization. Core ideology does not come from mimicking the values of other companies — even highly visionary companies; it does not come from following the dictates of outsiders; it does not come from reading management books; and it does not come from a sterile intellectual exercise of "calculating" what values would be most pragmatic, most popular, or most profitable. When articulating and codifying core ideology, the key step is to capture what is authentically believed, not what other companies set as their values or what the outside world thinks the ideology should be.

It's important to understand that core ideology exists as an internal element, largely independent of the external environment. To use an analogy, the founders of the United States didn't instill the core ideology of freedom and equality because the environment dictated it, nor did they expect the country to ever abandon those basic ideals in response to environmental conditions. They envisioned freedom and equality as timeless ideals independent of the environment ("We hold these truths to be self-evident...") — ideals to always work toward, providing guidance and inspiration to all future generations. The same holds true in visionary companies.

Robert W. Johnson, Jr. didn't write the credo because of a conceptual theory that linked credos with profits or because he read it in a book somewhere. He wrote the credo because the company embodied deeply held beliefs that he wanted to preserve. George Merck II deeply believed that medicine is for the patient, and he wanted every Merck person to share that belief. Thomas J. Watson, Jr. described IBM's core values as "bone deep" in his father: "As far as he was concerned, those values were the rules of life — to be preserved at all costs, to be commended to others, and to be followed conscientiously in one's business life."[5]

David Packard and Bill Hewlett didn't "plan" the HP Way or HP's "WHY of business," they simply held deep convictions about the way a business *should* be built and took tangible steps to articulate and disseminate these convictions so they could be preserved and acted upon. And they held these beliefs *independent* of the current management fashions of the day. In sifting through the Hewlett-Packard Company archives, we came across the following statement made by David Packard:

[In 1949], I attended a meeting of business leaders. I suggested at the meeting that management people had a responsibility beyond that of making a profit for their stockholders. I said that we ... had a responsibility to our employees to recognize their dignity as human beings, and to assure that they should share in the success which their work made possible. I pointed out, also, that we had a responsibility to our customers, and to the community at large, as well. I was surprised and shocked that not a single person at that meeting agreed with me. While they were reasonably polite in their disagreement, it was quite evident they firmly believed I was not one of them, and obviously not qualified to manage an important enterprise.[6]

Hewlett, Packard, Merck, Johnson, and Watson didn't sit down and ask "What business values would maximize our wealth?" or "What philosophy would look nice printed on glossy paper?" or "What beliefs would please the financial community?" No! They articulated what was inside them — what was in their gut, what was bone deep. It was as natural to them as breathing. It's not what they believed as much as *how deeply they believed it* (and how consistently their organizations lived it). Again, the key word is authenticity. No artificial flavors. No added sweeteners. Just 100 percent genuine authenticity.

FOOTNOTES:

[1] Thomas J. Watson, Jr., *A Business and Its Beliefs* (New York: Columbia University Press, 1963), 5-6, 72-73.

[2] Sam Walton with John Huey, *Sam Walton: Made in America* (New York: Doubleday, 1992), 183, 233.

[3] "Memorable Years in P&G History," company publication, 7.

[4] Author interview with John Young, 17 April 1992.

[5] Thomas J. Watson, Jr., *A Business and Its Beliefs* (New York: Columbia University Press, 1963), 12-13.

[6] David Packard, commencement speech, Colorado College, June 1, 1964, courtesy Hewlett-Packard Company archives.

XXIV

Values of
Long-Lived Companies
by Arie de Geus

In the early 80's, Shell commissioned a study to examine the questions of corporate longevity. They wanted to find out whether these companies had something in common that could explain why they were such successful survivors. They found four key factors in common:

1. Long-lived companies were sensitive to their environment. Whether they had built their fortunes on knowledge (such as DuPont's technological innovations) or on natural resources (such as the Hudson Bay Company's access to the furs of Canadian forests), they remained in harmony with the world around them. As wars, depressions, technologies, and political changes surged and ebbed around them, they always seemed to excel at keeping their feelers out, tuned to whatever was going on around them. They did this; it seemed, despite the fact that in the past there were little data available, let alone the communications facilities to give them a global view of the business environment. They sometimes had to rely for information on packets carried over vast distances by portage and ship. Moreover, societal considerations were rarely given prominence in the deliberations of company boards.

Yet they managed to react in timely fashion to the conditions of society around them.

2. Long-lived companies were cohesive, with a strong sense of identity. No matter how widely diversified they were, their employees (and even their suppliers, at times) felt they were all part of one entity. One company, Unilever, saw itself as a fleet of ships, each ship independent, yet the whole fleet stronger than the sum of its parts. This sense of belonging to an organization and being able to identify with its achievements can easily be dismissed as a "soft" or abstract feature of change. But case histories repeatedly showed that strong employee links were essential for survival amid change. This cohesion around the idea of "community" meant that managers were typically chosen for advancement from within; they succeeded through the generational flow of members and considered themselves stewards of the longstanding enterprise. Each management generation was only a link in a long chain. Except during conditions of crisis, the management's top priority and concern was the health of the institution as a whole.

3. Long-lived companies were tolerant. At first, when we wrote our Shell report, we called this point "decentralization." Long-lived companies, as we pointed out, generally avoided exercising any centralized control over attempts to diversify the company. Later, when I considered our research again, I realized that seventeenth-, eighteenth-, and nineteenth-century managers would never have used the word, *decentralized;* it was a twentieth-century invention. In what terms, then, would they have thought about their own company policies? As I studied the histories, I kept returning to the idea of "tolerance." These companies were particularly tolerant of activities on the margin: outliers, experiments, and eccentricities within the boundaries of the cohesive firm, which kept stretching their understanding of possibilities.

133

4. Long-lived companies were conservative in financing.
   They were frugal and did not risk their capital gratuitous-
   ly. They understood the meaning of money in an old-fashioned way; they knew the usefulness of having spare cash
   in the kitty. Having money in hand gave them flexibility
   and independence of action. They could pursue options
   that their competitors could not. They could grasp opportunities without first having to convince third-party
   financiers of their attractiveness.

It did not take us long to notice the factors that did *not* appear on
the list. The ability to return investment to shareholders seemed
to have nothing to do with longevity. The profitability of a company was a *symptom* of corporate health, but not a *predictor* or
determinant of corporate health. Certainly, a manager in a long-
lived company needed all the accounting figures that he or she
could lay hands on. But those companies seemed to recognize
that figures, even when accurate, describe the past. They do not
indicate the underlying conditions that will lead to deteriorating
health in the future. The financial reports at General Motors,
Philips Electronics, and IBM during the mid-1970S gave no
clue of the trouble that lay in store for those companies within
a decade. Once the problems cropped up on the balance sheet,
it was too late to prevent the trouble.

Nor did longevity seem to have anything to do with a company's material assets, its particular industry or product line, or its
country of origin. Indeed, the 40- to 50-year life expectancy seems
to be equally valid in countries as wide apart as the United States,
Europe, and Japan, and in industries ranging from manufacturing
to retailing to financial services to agriculture to energy.

At the time, we chose not to make the Shell study available
to the general public, and it still remains unpublished today. The
reasons had to do with the lack of scientific reliability for our
conclusions. Our sample of 30 companies was too small. Our
documentation was not always complete. And, as the management thinker Russell Ackoff once pointed out to me, our four key
factors represented a statistical correlation; our results should

therefore be treated with suspicion. Finally, as the authors of the study noted in their introduction, "Analysis, so far completed, raises considerable doubts about whether it is realistic to expect business history to give much guidance for business futures, given the extent of business environmental changes which have occurred during the present century."[1]

Nonetheless, our conclusions have recently received corroboration from a source with a great deal of academic respectability. Between 1988 and 1994, Stanford University professors James Collins and Jerry Porras asked 700 chief executives of U.S. companies — large and small, private and public, industrial and service — to name the firms they most admired. From the responses, they culled a list of 18 "visionary" companies. They didn't set out to find long-lived companies, but, as it happened, most of the firms that the CEOs chose had existed for 60 years or longer. (The only exceptions were Sony and Wal-Mart.) Collins and Porras paired these companies up with key competitors (Ford with General Motors, Procter & Gamble with Colgate, Motorola with Zenith) and began to look at the differences. The visionary companies put a lower priority on maximizing shareholder wealth or profits. Just as we had discovered, Collins and Porras found that their most-admired companies combined sensitivity to their environment with a strong sense of identity: "Visionary companies display a powerful drive for progress that enables them to change and adapt without compromising their cherished core ideals."[2]

At Shell, we never conducted any study of similar diligence. Nonetheless, the Shell study remained uppermost in my mind for years. In our unscientific way, we had found four characteristics that seemed, when put together, to give us a description of a highly successful type of company — a company that could survive for very long periods in an ever-changing world, because its managers were good at the management of change.

Defining the Living Company

Over time, the same four factors that we developed in our study of long-lived companies at Shell have continued to resonate in my mind. Gradually, they began to change my thinking about the real nature of companies — and of what it means for the way that we, managers at all levels, run those companies. I now see these four components this way:

1. *Sensitivity to the environment* represents a company's ability to learn and adapt.
2. *Cohesion and identity*, it is now clear, are aspects of a company's innate ability to build a community and a persona for itself.
3. *Tolerance* and its corollary, *decentralization*, are both symptoms of a company's awareness of ecology: its ability to build constructive relationships with other entities, within and outside itself.
4. And I now think of *conservative financing* as one element in a very critical corporate attribute: the ability to govern its own growth and evolution effectively.

Moreover, the question remains: Why would these same characteristics occur again and in companies that had managed to outlive others?

In a sense, I have been intrigued by these issues all of my working life, beginning with my time at university. I am convinced that the four characteristics of a long-lived company are not answers. They represent the start of a fundamental inquiry about the nature and success of commercial organizations and their role in the human community.

FOOTNOTES:

[1]   Royal Dutch Shell Group Planning PL/1, *Corporate Change: A Look at How Long-Established Companies Change*, September 1983, Appendix V, 25.

[2]   James C. Collins and Jerry I. Porras, *Built to Last: Successful Habits of Visionary Companies* (New York: HarperCollins, 1994), 9.

XXV
New Approaches
to Business
by Matthew Fox

Just as religion depends on theology for an ideological support system, so business depends often uncritically — on the economic ideology that underpins it. One can expect that a new wind will sweep over business when economics is subjected to the critique that it deserves as we move from the industrial era to a green era. Business is a practical application, a praxis, of an economic theory. As that theory undergoes transformation, so too will business.

However, transformation works the other way around as well. That is to say, as the *praxis* changes, so too might the theory change. As business people attempt to do business more from a creation-centered model, they will feed into the theoretical world of economics some new and refreshing approaches.

Examples of New Paradigm Approaches

Schumacher offers examples of new and *small* businesses that have sprung up, making intermediate technology available to people. One African village began manufacturing egg cartons in relatively modest numbers, with the result that an entire cottage industry of making egg cartons was established. (All previous manufacturers of egg cartons made them in quantities too great for small villagers' needs.) In Khurja, India, a town ninety miles from Delhi, there sprang up within a period of twelve years three hundred pottery factories employing 30,000 people to produce pottery and hospital and electrical porcelain.[1] This is an example of how people are already working with the new paradigm — putting people to work in small businesses that remain simple and people centered.

Another example closer to home is the business of Ben Cohen and Jerry Greenfield, the inventors of Ben and Jerry's ice cream. Their corporation, which has grown into a ninety-million-dollar business, is committed to donating 7.5 percent of pretax earnings to nonprofit organizations. (Most corporations give less than 1 percent of pretax earnings to charity.) They deliberately support family farmers by paying more than the government recommends for milk; they use their packaging to advertise value-oriented issues pertaining to peace and the environment. They consciously contribute to defending the rain forest by purchasing Brazil nuts from people in the rain forests and calling their product "rain forest crunch" in order to raise consciousness about the rain forest.

Ironically, Cohen and Greenfield were at first so taken aback by their success that they were ready to sell their business. Instead, they took up the challenge of changing business. Along the way they ran into the business world's perhaps inevitable resistance. (All persons wishing to reinvent work can expect to encounter such resistance. It ought not to discourage us, as it did not discourage Ben and Jerry. Thomas Kuhn points out that resistance is one of the signs of a paradigm shift.)

Cohen and Greenfield deliberately changed their way of doing business. Instead of the old-paradigm definition of business, "An entity that produces a product or provides a service," they coined a new slogan: "Organized human energy plus money will produce power." Business may be "the most powerful force in the world," Ben proposes, and as such it needs to accept the responsibility that goes with power. Business is a focused energy, like a laser, that in fact sets the tone for a society. He asks the question: "Does business have a value *beyond* maximizing profits?" After all, individuals have values but are often told on coming to work to leave their values at the door. At work, "we are prevented from acting on our values," he contends. "If individuals have a responsibility to help the community, we cannot possibly suspend that responsibility just when we're at our most effective, that is, when we are at work." Ben asks why it is that business lacks values. It is because of an ideology we carry with us from the old paradigm, namely that one "can't make profits and help the community at the same time." The result of such a dogma is that the environment, the workers, and the community all suffer at the hands of the workplace."[2]

It is the experience of Ben and Jerry that this tired shibboleth creating a dualism between work and values simply no longer works.

> As long as we operate within this old paradigm, we are separated from our heart and values and feel powerless. We cannot suspend our values during the workday and think we will have them back when we get home. We're all interconnected. There is a spiritual dimension to business just as to individuals![3]

Notice how Ben is invoking one of the new laws of the universe (an old one to mystics): interconnection. He sees the suffering we rain on one another as due to a lack of interconnection. Like Schumacher, Ben and Jerry criticize business for being so insular and narrowly focused on one ingredient: the quantitative. "The only measure for business," Ben points out, "is quantitative. It is only about profit and loss." In this regard Ben is critiquing the mechanistic and quantitatively-oriented worldview of the Newtonian era when what counted was exclusively what was quantifiable?[4]

Redefining the Bottom Line

In a conscious effort to break out of this confining and unrealistic paradigm, Ben and Jerry have redefined the bottom line in business. Instead of asking *only,* "How much profit do we have at the end of the year?" they now also ask, "How much have we helped the community of which we are a part?" The question is decidedly *not* an issue of philanthropy but "the way we do business." And so they have introduced into their business a yearly report called an "Audited Social Statement." They undergo two audits each year — a financial one and a social one. They have found that the latter "is good for business," for "the community supports that business that supports the community." Profit is a regulator of business *but not the only one*. Other human factors must also be taken into account. When these are lacking, then business takes a "narrow, selfish" stand on political issues. "Business", says Ben, "needs to integrate community care into its way of operating." In other words, business must join the revolution taking place around the Great Work of the universe — the work from which business, and all human endeavor, will derive its meaning and its rules. Business must become interdependent; that is, it must relate to the greater community around it, listening to its pain and its joys.[5]

Some ways in which Ben and Jerry's have reached out to the greater community are as follows:

- They went public with the company in order to invite the community to become co-owners of the business. They did this by offering stock at 126 dollars per share so that ordinary folks could afford it. The result has been that one of everyone hundred families in the state of Vermont, where the business is located, owns stock in their company.
- The materials they use in their product are chosen from communities that support the oppressed. For example, baked goods are ordered from Buddhist communities that hire the homeless and train them to be bakers; coffee is bought from a Mexican coffee cooperative; blueberries come from next-door small farmers in Maine; nuts come from the rain forest.
- Their shops are used as polling places, and their managers are authorized as notaries to do voter registration, so as to get persons to vote on the spot when they come in for ice cream (when you register you get a free ice cream cone).

- They hire homeless to sell their products.
- They intend to reduce their energy consumption by 25 percent within ten years by solar power and other ways.
- They chose the South Shore Bank of Chicago as their bank. That bank, located in a decaying urban area, is committed to *greenlining,* or putting its money into the local neighborhood. Recently Ben and Jerry's has announced that they will build a factory in the heart of South Central Los Angeles. This factory will employ over two hundred local citizens.[6]

Ben is the first to point out that other businesses are also following this path: Patagonia, makers of outdoor clothing; Seventh Generation, manufacturers and distributors of environmentally healthy products; Working Assets, a socially responsible investment firm; Levi Strauss; Stridrite Shoes; Aveda, makers of hair and beauty products; and others. In addition, networks are developing around these new business paradigms: One Per Cent for Peace (to which over one hundred groups belong); Social Venture Network (over two hundred businesses); New England Business Association for Social Responsibility (one hundred members); and the national Business Association for Social Responsibility in Washington, D.C., which is launching an alternative chamber of commerce.

These organizations are dedicated to encouraging businesses to take responsibility for healthy and productive workplaces, for quality and environmental impact of their products and services, for community involvement (New England Businesses for Social Responsibility), and to use business to "create a more just, humane and environmentally sustainable society" (Social Venture Network). The approximately 2,000 committed companies in the social responsibility movement here and abroad have combined annual sales of $2 billion. This represents only one-hundredth of 1 percent of the sales volume of business enterprises world over. It would seem that business people are not all lagging behind in the effort to reinvent their work.

MATTHEW FOX

FOOTNOTES:

1. Schumacher, Good Work, 136, 137.
2. Ben Cohen, Choices for the Future.
3. Cohen, Choices for the Future.
4. Cohen, Choices for the Future.
5. Cohen, Choices for the Future.
6. Cohen, Choices for the Future.

About the Authors

Collins, Jim

Jim Collins is a student and teacher of enduring great companies — how they grow, how they attain superior performance, and how good companies can become great companies. Having invested over a decade of research into the topic, Jim has authored or co-authored four books, including the classic *Built to Last*, a fixture on the *Business Week* best seller list for more than six years, and has been translated into 29 languages. His work has been featured in *Fortune*, *The Wall Street Journal*, *Business Week*, *Harvard Business Review*, and *Fast Company*.

Csikszentmihalyi, Mihaly

Mihaly Csikszentmihalyi is currently Professor at the Drucker School of Management at Claremont Graduate University in Claremont, California and former Professor and Chairman of the Department of Psychology at the University of Chicago. His previous books include the best selling *Flow*, *Being Adolescent*, *The Evolving Self*, *Creativity*, *Finding Flow and Becoming Adult*. He lives in Claremont, California.

Damon, William

William Damon is Professor of Education at Stanford University and Senior Fellow at the Hoover Institution on War, Revolution, and Peace. His books include *The Moral Child*; *Some Do Care: Contemporary Lives of Moral Commitment*; *Greater Expectations*; *Good Work: When Excellence and Ethics Meet* and *Noble Purpose: The Joys of Living a Meaningful Life*.

De Geus, Arie

Arie De Geus worked for Royal Dutch/Shell for 38 years. Widely credited with originating the concept of the learning organization, he is a visiting fellow at the London Business School and a board member of the MIT Center for Organizational learning.

Ealy, Diane, C.

C. Diane Ealy is a writer, speaker, and healer who is devoted to facilitating personal growth in herself and others. She holds a Ph.D. in behavioral science, specializing in the feminine creative process. Her spiritual development has always been a part of Diane's journey to the Self so writing a book describing how to respond spiritually in the workplace was a natural for her. Diane enjoys communicating her message of personal growth through speeches and workshops, individual sessions, and writing.

Fox, Matthew

Matthew Fox is author of 28 books including *Original Blessing, The Reinvention of Work, Creativity: Where the Divine and the Human Meet, One River, Many Wells: Wisdom Springing from Global Faiths, A Spirituality Named Compassion* and his most recent *A New Reformation!* He was a member of the Dominican Order for 34 years. He holds a doctorate (received summa cum laude) in the History and Theology of Spirituality from the Institut Catholique de Paris. He is currently lecturing, teaching and writing and is President of the non-profit that he created in 1984, Friends of Creation Spirituality.

Gardner, Howard

Howard Garner is Hobbs Professor of Cognition and Education, Chairman of the Steering Committee of Project Zero at the Harvard Graduate School of Education, and Adjunct Professor of Neurology at the Boston University School of Medicine. He is the author of eighteen books, including *Frames of Mind, Creating Minds, Leading Minds, Multiple Intelligence* and *Intelligence Reframed*. He lives in Cambridge, Massachusetts.

Kiel, Fred

Fred Kiel, Ph. D., co-founder of KRW International Inc. brings over 30 years of experience to his work with Fortune 500 CEOs and senior executives on building organizational effectiveness through leadership excellence and aligning organization with mission. Kiel is often called the "father of executive coaching" for his pioneering work in this field. Before founding KRW, Kiel worked with senior executives in private practice, developing a rigorous data-gathering and customized development process designed to provide executives with transformative feedback.

Kuczmarski, Susan Smith

Susan Smith Kuczmarski, Ed.D., is an educator, lecturer, and authority on the dynamics of family culture. Trained as a social scientist, Dr. Kuczmarski has done extensive research on how children learn social skills and how adolescents become leaders. During the course of a career spanning 30 years, she has developed and conducted workshops and programs for educators, parents, and teenagers, including inter-school workshops on coping with the demands of greater responsibility for younger teens, leadership-building retreats for high school teens, and workshops and seminars devoted to helping college teens sort through their values and future directions. She holds a Doctorate in Education from Columbia University in New York City, where she was named an International Fellow.

Kuczmarski, Thomas

Thomas Kuczmarski, Senior Partner and President of Kuczmarski & Associates, is a nationally recognized expert in the management of new products and services innovation, and marketing strategy. During his career of helping hundreds of companies grow their businesses, his leading-edge work has forged a new meaning for "innovation" throughout corporate America. His extensive work in advising clients on leadership in innovation serves as the foundation for the firm's values-based leadership expertise. He has successfully developed new products and business strategies for a comprehensive range of industries, from small businesses to Fortune 100 corporations. Mr. Kuczmarski is an Adjunct Professor of New Products and Services at Northwestern University's Kellogg Graduate School of Management and The University of Chicago Graduate School of Business.

Lennick, Doug

Doug Lennick is co-founder and managing partner of The Lennick Aberman Group. He is legendary for his innovative approaches to developing high performance in individuals and organizations. Before founding The Lennick Aberman Group, Lennick was Executive Vice President-Advice and Retail Distribution for American Express Financial Advisors (AEFA) in that capacity, he led an organization of 17,000 field and corporate associates to unprecedented success. Lennick is co-author of the highly regarded book, *Moral Intelligence: Enhancing Business Performance and Leadership Success.* He is currently a member of the prestigious Consortium for Research on Emotional Intelligence in Organizations. In addition, Lennick is a Fellow at the Carlson Executive Development Center, Carlson School of Management at the University of Minnesota.

Pillai, Radhakrishnan

The founder Director of Atma Darshan, Radhakrishnan Pillai has over 13 years experience in the fields of marketing and logistics. He has done an extensive management research course on Kautilya's *Arthaśāstra*, the first book on Management written nearly 2000 years ago by Chankaya, the world's first Management Guru. He is currently working on PhD in this subject. He has been an active member of the Chinmaya Mission for over 18 years. His deep interest in the study and research of the ancient Indian scriptures have led to discovery of various management principles applicable in today's corporate world.

Porras, Jerry, I.

Jerry I. Porras is the Lane Professor of Organizational Behavior and Change, Emeritus, at the Stanford University Graduate School of Business where he served as an Associate Dean for Academic Affairs and frequent executive education teacher. He studies ways of aligning companies around their purpose and core values to produce lasting high performance.

Premji, Azim

Azim Premji is a distinguished Indian businessman. He is a graduate in Electrical Engineering from Stanford University, USA. At the age of 21, Premji joined Wipro, then his father's vegetable oil business after the sudden demise of his father. Now he is the Chairman of Wipro Corporation. A role model for young entrepreneurs across the world, Mr. Azim Premji has integrated the country's entrepreneurial tradition with professional management, based on sound values and uncompromising integrity.

Richmond, Lewis

Lewis Richmond is a Buddhist teacher and author, software entrepreneur, and musician/composer. He was the founder and owner of Forerunner Systems Inc, the leading provider of inventory management software to the catalog industry. An ordained disciple of Buddhist master Shunryu Suzuki Roshi, Lewis co-leads the Vimala Sangha, a meditation group in Mill Valley, California.

Spears, Nancy

Nancy Spears is the author of a new book that offers profound ways to integrate value-based leadership into Corporate America, *Buddha: 9 to 5: The Eightfold Path to Enlightening Your Workplace and Improving Your Bottom Line*. Founder and CEO of a national marketing and production agency with offices in seven cities coast to coast, Nancy's marketing expertise includes providing strategic marketing communications counsel and services to Fortune 500 companies who value quality of thinking, execution, and service.

Swami Atmashraddhananda

A Monk of the Ramakrishna Order, the author presently edits *The Vedanta Kesari*, the spiritual monthly published from Sri Ramakrishna Math, Chennai. He is also associated with various youth groups and occasionally gives lectures on the life and teachings of Swami Vivekananda and the Upanishads.

Swami Chinmayananda

His Holiness Swami Chinmayananda, founder of Chinmaya Mission, taught spirituality as the art of living. Through *jñana yoga* (the Vedantic path of spiritual knowledge), he emphasized the balance of head and heart, pointing out selfless work, study, and meditation as the cornerstones of spiritual practice. Not satisfied by worldly aspirations or his degrees in literature and law, Balakrishna Menon pursued spiritual studies for nine years in the Himalayas, under the guidance of Swami Sivananda (Divine Life Society) and the tutelage of Swami Tapovanam. He eventually came to share this Vedantic knowledge with the masses, in the form of the dynamic teacher known as Swami Chinmayananda. Swamiji is renowned worldwide as a spiritual master and one of the foremost teachers of *Bhagavad Gītā*. He is credited with the renaissance of spirituality and cultural values in India, and with the spreading of the ageless wisdom of *Advaita Vedānta,* as expounded by Adi Shankaracharya, throughout the world. Swami Chinmayananda attained *mahāsamādhi* in August 1993. His legacy remains in the form of written, audio, and video publications; social service projects; Vedanta teachers whom he taught and inspired; and Chinmaya Mission centers worldwide, serving the spiritual and cultural needs of local communities.

Swami Jyotirmayananda

Swami Jyotirmayananda was born on February 3, 1931 in Bihar, India. He embraced the ancient order of *saṁnyāsa* on February 3, 1953 at the age of 22. He served his guru, Swami Sivananda tirelessly. In March 1969 he established an ashram in Miami Florida, the Yoga Research Foundation that has become the center for international activities. Branches of this organization now exist throughout the world.

Swami Nikhilananda

While studying for a Masters degree in Geology at St. Xavier's College Mumbai, Swami Nikhilananda took the momentous decision of changing the direction of his life. Following an inner calling Swami Nikhilananda quit formal education and joined the Vedanta course at the Mumbai Ashram of the Chinmaya Mission in the year 1984. He spent two and half years in intense study of the scriptures under the guidance of Swami Tejomayananda, the present head of the Chinmaya Mission. He also had the good fortune to learn Vedantic texts directly from Swami Chinmayananda. Presently he is the spiritual head of Chinmaya Mission New Delhi, Noida, and Gurgaon. He is actively involved in the various activities and projects of the Mission. He also oversees and manages the affairs of two Chinmaya Vidyalayas and a Chinmaya Degree College.

Swami Tejomayananda

Swami Tejomayananda, the spiritual head of Chinmaya Mission centers worldwide since 1993, is fulfilling the vision of his guru, Swami Chinmayananda. As Mission head, Swami Tejomayananda has already conducted more than 450 *jñāna yajña* worldwide. He has served as dean or *ācārya* of the Sandeepany Institutes of Vedanta, both in India and in California. Fluent in Hindi, Marathi, and English, and lecturing and writing commentaries in all three languages, he makes even the most complicated Vedantic topics clear to his audience. Swamiji excels in expounding upon a wide spectrum of Hindu scriptures, from *Rāmāyaṇa*, to *Bhagavad Gītā*, to the Upanishads. His easy manner, combined with his in-depth analyses and devotional renderings of Vedantic texts, have drawn many newcomers into the spiritual fold.

Tolle, Eckhart

Eckhart Tolle is widely recognized as one of the most original and inspiring spiritual teachers of our time. He travels and teaches throughout the world. Eckhart is not aligned with any particular religion or tradition, but excludes none. At the core of his teachings lies the transformation of individual and collective human consciousness — a global spiritual awakening. Eckhart was born in Germany and educated at the Universities of London and Cambridge. At the age of twenty-nine, a profound spiritual transformation virtually dissolved his old identity and radically changed the course of his life. Eckhart Tolle is the author of *The Power of Now* a #1 New York Times Bestseller, which has been translated into 32 languages and become one of the most influential spiritual books of our time.

Sanskrit Pronunciation Guide

a	f**u**n	i	p**i**n	om	f**oam**
ā	c**a**r	ī	f**ee**t	p	**p**urse
ai	h**igh**	j	**j**ug	ph	sap**ph**ire
au	c**ow**	jh	he**dg**ehog	r	**r**un
b	b**u**t	jñ	**no equiva-**	ṛ	**r**ig
bh	a**bh**or	k	**k**ind	ṝ	long **ṛ**
c	**ch**unk	kh	bloc**kh**ead	s	**s**ir
ch	ma**tch**	kṣ	wor**ksh**eet	ś	**sh**ovel
d	fea**th**er	l	**l**uck	ṣ	bu**sh**el
dh	wi**th**er	ḷ	wor**l**d	t	**t**hink
ḍ	**d**uck	m	**m**other	th	pa**th**etic
ḍh	god-**h**ood	ṁ	**see below**	ṭ	**t**ouch
e	pl**ay**	n	**n**umber	ṭh	an**th**ill
g	**g**ate	ṇ	thu**n**der	tr	**tr**ee
gh	log-**h**ut	ṅ	si**ng**	u	p**u**t
h	**h**ouse	ñ	bu**n**ch	ū	p**oo**l
ḥ	**see below**	o	**o**ver	v	**v**irtue
				y	**y**oung

ḥ	aspiration of preceding consonant
ṁ	nasalization of preceding consonant
'	unpronounced a
"	unpronounced ā (long a)

The Sanskrit word *Mananam* means reflection. The *Mananam Series* of books is dedicated to promoting the ageless wisdom of Vedanta, with an emphasis on the unity of all religions. Spiritual teachers from different traditions give us fresh, insightful answers to age-old questions so that we may apply them in a practical way to the dilemmas we all face in life. It is published by Chinmaya Mission West, which was founded by Swami Chinmayananda in 1975. Swami Chinmayananda pursued the spiritual path in the Himalayas, under the guidance of Swami Sivananda and Swami Tapovanam. He is credited with the awakening of India and the rest of the world to the ageless wisdom of Vedanta. He taught the logic of spirituality and emphasized that selfless work, study, and meditation are the cornerstones of spiritual practice. His legacy remains in the form of books, audio and video tapes, schools, social service projects, and Vedanta teachers who now serve their local communities all around the world.